UNDERSTANDING SCIENCE & NATURE

Evolution of Life

TIME-LIFE
ALEXANDRIA, VIRGINIA

C O N T E N T S

5 The Humans Arrive

6 Scientific Proofs of Evolution

1

The Evolution of Species

The oldest known living creature, a bacterium, took form in the Earth's oceans some 3.5 billion years ago. In the eons since, life has become tremendously diverse. Living organisms now include as many as 30 million species occupying nearly every nook and cranny on Earth. Each species is unique, possessing some trait that sets it apart from all other forms of life. Yet every species—the worms that endure precariously at the bottom of the ocean, the insects that live in the treetops of the tropical rain forest, the tiniest bacterium, the largest redwood tree, the hem-

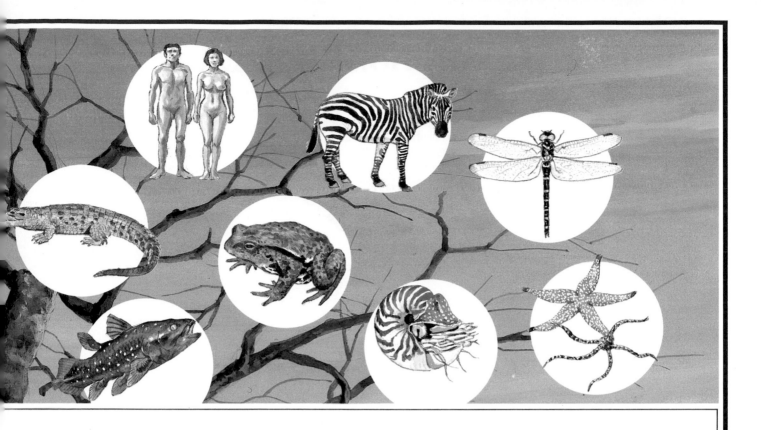

lock, and the human being—can trace its origin back to a common, single-celled ancestor. The process by which this transformation occurred is known as evolution.

A new species evolves as it responds to changing conditions on Earth. The planet is a hostile place, yet it offers many environments in which a species can find nourishment, grow, and produce offspring better than any other species can. Each species, in fact, fills each niche better as it evolves. This process, known as adaptation, channels evolution.

Conditions on Earth change over time, however—ice ages come and go, for example—and an entrenched species may not be able to adapt to its new environment. If so, it may become extinct. Or else, natural selection may act to change a species' adaptations, and in time, a new species may appear. Evolution occurs and the diversity of life increases.

Evolution follows a pattern that resembles the branching of an old tree. At each branch, diversity increases.

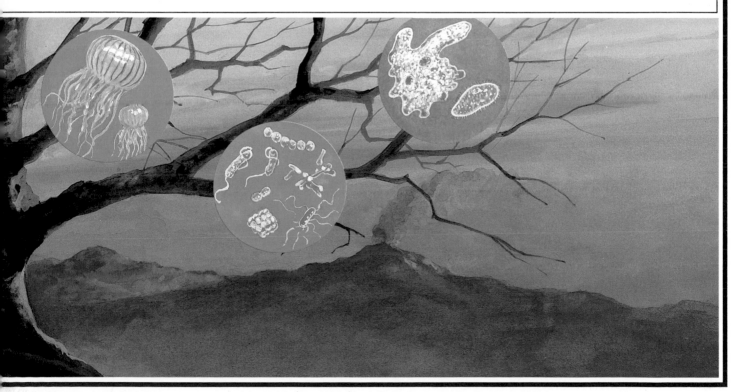

What Does Evolution Look Like?

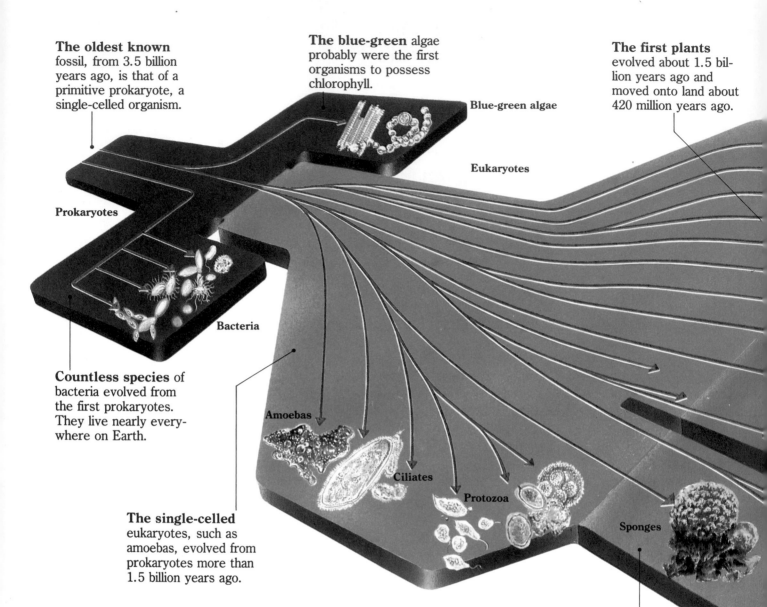

The oldest known fossil, from 3.5 billion years ago, is that of a primitive prokaryote, a single-celled organism.

The blue-green algae probably were the first organisms to possess chlorophyll.

The first plants evolved about 1.5 billion years ago and moved onto land about 420 million years ago.

Blue-green algae

Eukaryotes

Prokaryotes

Bacteria

Countless species of bacteria evolved from the first prokaryotes. They live nearly everywhere on Earth.

Amoebas

Ciliates

Protozoa

Sponges

The single-celled eukaryotes, such as amoebas, evolved from prokaryotes more than 1.5 billion years ago.

Sponges, which evolved 570 million years ago, are the simplest members of the animal kingdom because they do not possess distinct organs. There are more than 5,000 species of sponge.

Classifying life

Biologists give each living thing a scientific name that classifies it, showing its relationship to other living things. The basic unit of classification is the species. Closely related species, those sharing an immediate common ancestor, belong to the same genus. For example, cherries, plums, peaches, and flowering almonds *(right)* all belong to the same genus. Related genuses belong to a family, related families belong to an order, and so on through subclasses, classes, phyla, and finally the kingdoms. Each higher level of classification represents an earlier stage of evolution. There are fewer divisions at each level, so while there are millions of species, there are only five kingdoms.

Cherry

Damson plum

Flowering almond

Peach

Plum

Species	
Genus	Prunus
Family	Rosaceae
Order	Rosa florae
Subclass	Chlorypetalae
Class	Dicotyledoneae
Kingdom	Plant

The pattern of evolution resembles a tree, with the end of each branch representing a species. When a branch splits, life becomes more diverse.

One of the first splits in evolutionary history occurred when the eukaryotes—organisms with complex cells—evolved from the prokaryotes, simple single-celled organisms. Other major branches appeared when multicelled eukaryotes evolved from the single-celled eukaryotes, and when the plant and animal kingdoms separated. At each split, some trait appeared that distinguished one group of organisms from another. Closely related species—those sharing many traits—sit near each other on the tree of life.

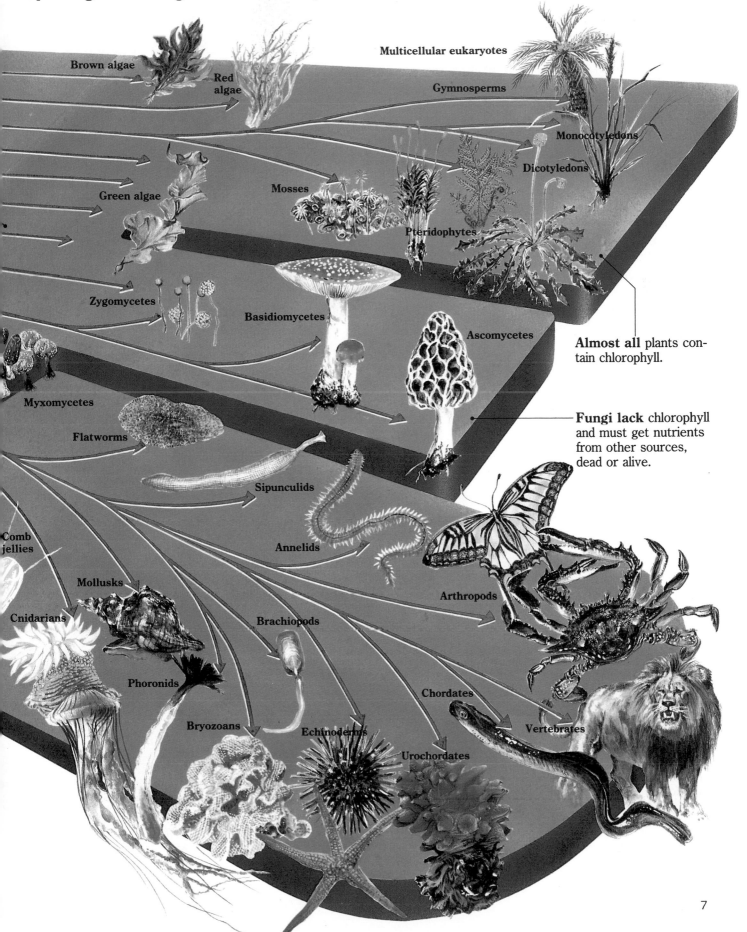

Brown algae

Red algae

Multicellular eukaryotes

Gymnosperms

Monocotyledons

Dicotyledons

Green algae

Mosses

Pteridophytes

Zygomycetes

Basidiomycetes

Ascomycetes

Almost all plants contain chlorophyll.

Myxomycetes

Flatworms

Fungi lack chlorophyll and must get nutrients from other sources, dead or alive.

Sipunculids

Annelids

Comb jellies

Mollusks

Arthropods

Cnidarians

Brachiopods

Phoronids

Chordates

Bryozoans

Echinoderms

Vertebrates

Urochordates

How Many Species Are There?

Few creatures that lived on Earth's surface in the planet's first 4 billion years are preserved as fossils. Around 600 million years ago, animals with hard structures emerged as the environment became more hospitable. These creatures left a fossil record. Millions of new species appeared and disappeared as evolution brought about the rise and fall of entire families of plants and animals.

Today biologists have identified nearly 1.5 million living species, but millions of others, mostly insects and microorganisms, have yet to be counted. The final total of species alive today may be as high as 30 million. Insects represent the largest phylum in the animal kingdom, in terms of numbers of species, and flowering plants are the most diverse division in the plant kingdom. With so many species on the planet, it is not surprising that life is found everywhere *(right),* from the tropics to the poles to the deepest oceans.

Ebb and flow of animals

Evolution does not occur smoothly over time. For example, the Cambrian period *(right)* saw an explosion in the number of animal families alive. In contrast, there was large extinction of animal families in the Ordovician period. When large numbers of species become extinct, many new ones will appear to take over their roles. Because of large-scale extinctions, some species living today have few if any close relatives alive. In some instances, the only trace of entire families of species is the fossils they left behind.

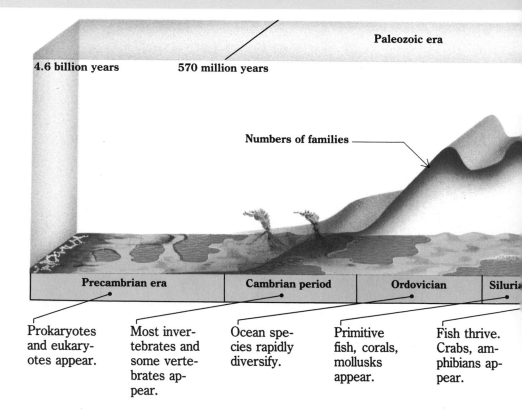

4.6 billion years **570 million years** **Paleozoic era**

Numbers of families

Precambrian era	Cambrian period	Ordovician	Siluria
Prokaryotes and eukaryotes appear.	Most invertebrates and some vertebrates appear.	Ocean species rapidly diversify.	Primitive fish, corals, mollusks appear.

Fish thrive. Crabs, amphibians appear.

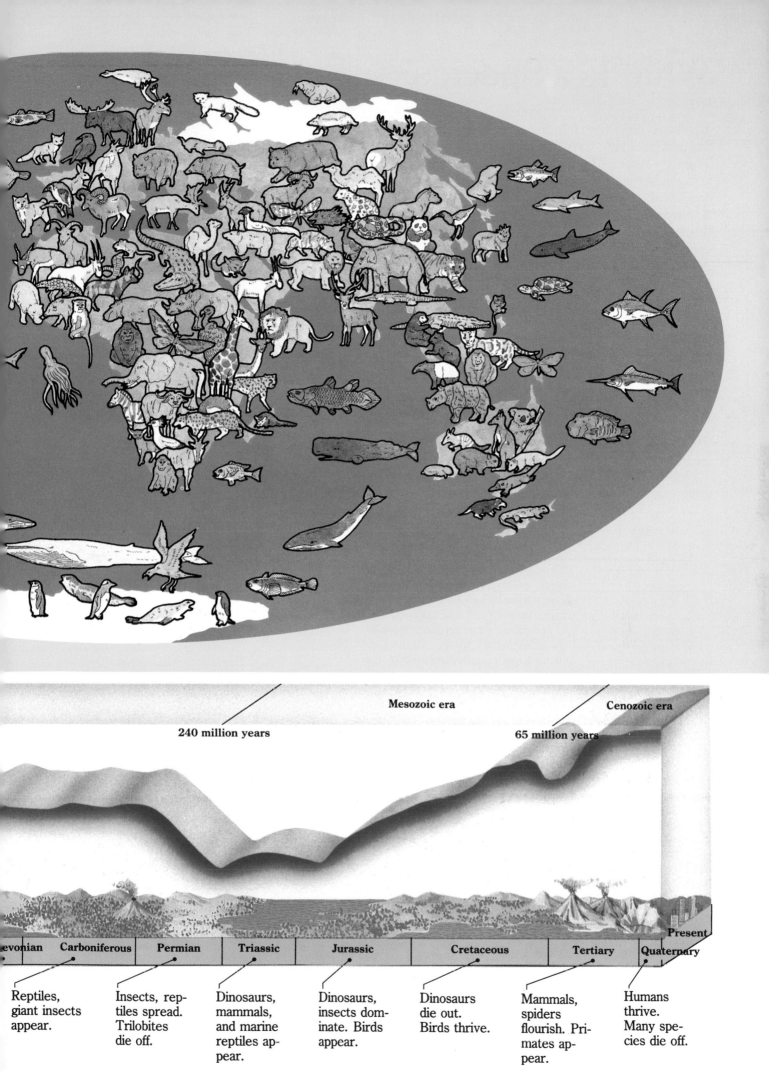

| evonian | Carboniferous | Permian | Triassic | Jurassic | Cretaceous | Tertiary | Quaternary |

Mesozoic era

240 million years

Cenozoic era

65 million years

Present

Reptiles, giant insects appear.

Insects, reptiles spread. Trilobites die off.

Dinosaurs, mammals, and marine reptiles appear.

Dinosaurs, insects dominate. Birds appear.

Dinosaurs die out. Birds thrive.

Mammals, spiders flourish. Primates appear.

Humans thrive. Many species die off.

What Is a Species?

The basic unit that biologists use to classify the millions of life forms on Earth is species. The key feature that unites members of a species is the fact that they can breed with one another and produce offspring that can also mate and produce young. In this way, the pieces of genetic information unique to each species are passed along to successive generations. In some cases members of closely related species, such as a horse and donkey, can mate. The offspring, in this case a mule, can be healthy but is almost always sterile, unable to breed.

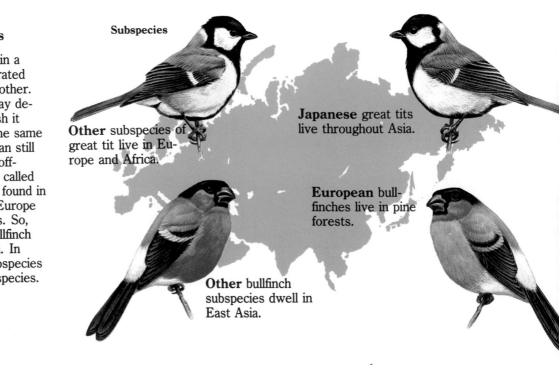

Lioness

Lion

● Breeding within a species

When a male and a female lion mate *(above, right)*, each passes along half of its genetic information to its offspring. Because the mates are of the same species, the two sets of genetic information are compatible, and the offspring are fertile. Future generations receive this genetic information, too.

Species and subspecies

Different populations within a species can become separated geographically from each other. Over time, each group may develop traits that distinguish it from other members of the same species, but the groups can still mate and produce fertile offspring. These groups are called subspecies. The great tit found in Asia and the great tit of Europe *(right, top)* are subspecies. So, too, are the European bullfinch and the Pyrrhula bullfinch. In time, however, these subspecies may evolve into distinct species.

Subspecies

Other subspecies of great tit live in Europe and Africa.

Japanese great tits live throughout Asia.

European bullfinches live in pine forests.

Other bullfinch subspecies dwell in East Asia.

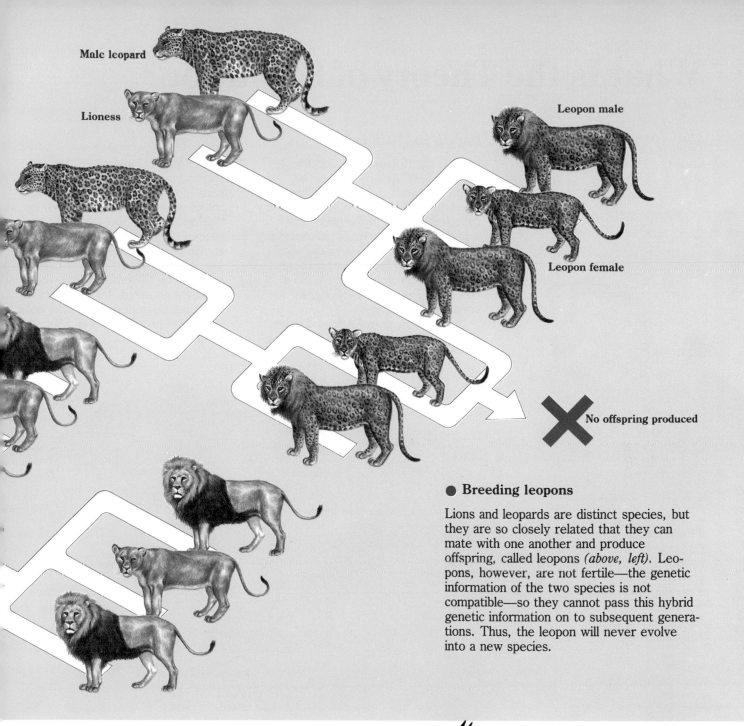

Male leopard

Lioness

Leopon male

Leopon female

✗ No offspring produced

● Breeding leopons

Lions and leopards are distinct species, but they are so closely related that they can mate with one another and produce offspring, called leopons *(above, left)*. Leopons, however, are not fertile—the genetic information of the two species is not compatible—so they cannot pass this hybrid genetic information on to subsequent generations. Thus, the leopon will never evolve into a new species.

Breeds of species

Humans have learned how to mate selected members of one species to produce a particular set of traits. Often, these matings can produce offspring that look far different from their ancestors but are still members of the same species and are called breeds. The genetic difference between breeds is minute, far less than the differences that distinguish two subspecies. The Afghan hound and the Chihuahua *(right),* for example, are breeds of the species *Canis familiaris*. These animals can mate and produce fertile (but funny-looking) young.

Breeds

Doberman pinscher

Bulldog

Pomeranian

Afghan hound

Chihuahua

Akita

What Is the Theory of Evolution?

**Charles Darwin
(1809-1882)**

Darwin and HMS *Beagle*

In 1835 the British naval ship *Beagle* reached the Galápagos Islands off South America's west coast. There, a young biologist named Charles Darwin collected samples of the plants and animals and took notes of his observations. Darwin was awed by the enormous variety of life inhabiting these islands and concluded that life must be ever changing, or evolving, to create such diversity.

Upon returning to England, Darwin spent 20 years studying his Galápagos Islands samples and notes. He observed variations among local populations of a species and saw that local conditions acted to select the traits that enabled one population of the species to survive better than another. He decided that it was in this way, through the process of natural selection by the environment, that evolution occurred. In 1859 Darwin published his conclusions in the book *On the Origin of Species by Means of Natural Selection.*

The animals of the Galápagos Islands *(shown at right, with current Spanish and older English names)* are similar to those of the South American mainland.

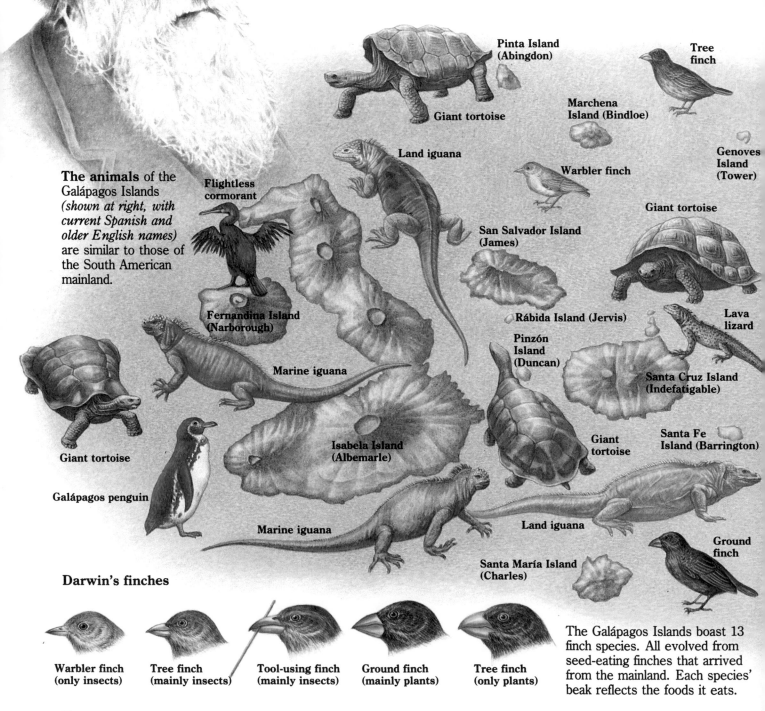

Pinta Island (Abingdon)

Giant tortoise

Tree finch

Marchena Island (Bindloe)

Land iguana

Warbler finch

Genoves Island (Tower)

Giant tortoise

San Salvador Island (James)

Flightless cormorant

Fernandina Island (Narborough)

Marine iguana

Rábida Island (Jervis)

Pinzón Island (Duncan)

Lava lizard

Santa Cruz Island (Indefatigable)

Santa Fe Island (Barrington)

Giant tortoise

Giant tortoise

Galápagos penguin

Marine iguana

Isabela Island (Albemarle)

Land iguana

Ground finch

Santa María Island (Charles)

Darwin's finches

Warbler finch (only insects)

Tree finch (mainly insects)

Tool-using finch (mainly insects)

Ground finch (mainly plants)

Tree finch (only plants)

The Galápagos Islands boast 13 finch species. All evolved from seed-eating finches that arrived from the mainland. Each species' beak reflects the foods it eats.

Naturalists beginning with Aristotle have known that organisms fall into groups that progress from simple to complex. It wasn't until the 19th century, however, that Charles Darwin developed the modern theory of evolution, successfully explaining how more complex species arose over time from simpler ones.

There are three important ideas in Darwin's theory. First, not all individuals of a species are identical—natural variation exists in their size or coloration, for example. Second, offspring can inherit these variations from their parents. Third, the natural environment puts pressure on an organism to survive and thus selects the traits that give a competitive advantage to one individual of a species over another.

Lamarck's theory of organic evolution

French biologist Jean-Baptiste Lamarck believed that the traits an organism acquired during its life passed to its offspring. For example, he assumed that modern giraffes *(below)* have long necks because their ancestors stretched their necks to reach leaves. However, modern biologists believe that acquired traits cannot be passed on.

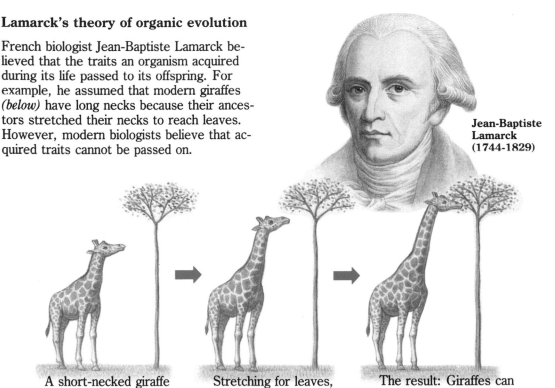

Jean-Baptiste Lamarck (1744-1829)

A short-necked giraffe couldn't reach food.

Stretching for leaves, the giraffe's neck grew.

The result: Giraffes can now reach high leaves.

Ground finch

Galápagos sea lion

San Cristóbal Island (Chatham)

Marine iguana

Española Island (Hood)

Cactus ground finch

Gregor Mendel's peas

Gregor Mendel, an Austrian monk, discovered the laws of genetics by studying how traits in peas were passed from one generation to the next *(right)*. Genetics explains part of the mechanism for evolution.

Gregor Johann Mendel (1822-1884)

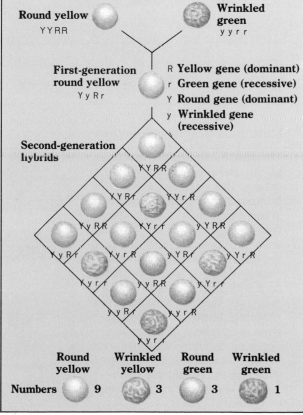

Round yellow
YYRR

Wrinkled green
y y r r

First-generation round yellow
Yy Rr

R Yellow gene (dominant)
r Green gene (recessive)
Y Round gene (dominant)
y Wrinkled gene (recessive)

Second-generation hybrids

	Round yellow	Wrinkled yellow	Round green	Wrinkled green
Numbers	9	3	3	1

Do Mutations Lead to Evolution?

Evolution can occur because variations exist within a species. These variations result from gene recombination during reproduction and from tiny changes, called mutations, that arise in an organism's genes, the units of genetic information passed from parent to offspring. Mutations are rare: They usually occur when a mistake is made in copying a cell's genes. Some mutations create neutral traits, ones that neither improve nor harm an organism's fitness, and these produce variation. But most mutations produce traits that reduce an organism's ability to survive in its environment. If conditions change, however, the mutation might give the organism an advantage. In that case, natural selection will eventually lead to evolution.

The mutation that makes this rainbow trout blue is linked to another, lethal mutation. If two blue trout mate, the offspring will die.

With normal markings a rainbow trout can hide from predators. The markings also identify it to other trout.

Mutations in *Drosophila* flies

The fruit fly *Drosophila* breeds quickly and produces many offspring. This lets geneticists study how a mutated gene is passed on. When a fruit fly with a mutation that produces short, or vestigial, wings mates with a normal fly, all the offspring have normal wings *(right)*. Vestigial wings are said to be a recessive trait, and normal wings are the dominant trait. The offspring, however, has one gene from each parent, and thus one dominant and one recessive gene. When these flies mate, one of every four offspring has two recessive genes and vestigial wings.

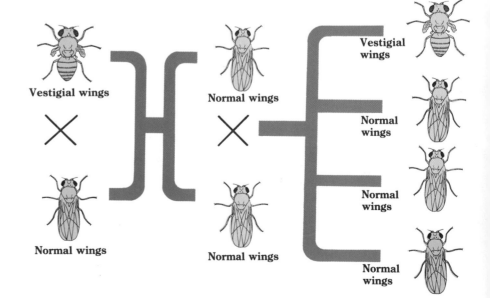

Vestigial wings × Normal wings

Normal wings × Normal wings

Vestigial wings

Normal wings

Normal wings

Normal wings

This rainbow trout's yellow color makes it an easy target for predators. It will have a difficult time surviving and breeding.

A mutation produces a trout with no stripes and dots. Other trout will not recognize it, so it will have little chance to breed.

What Is Natural Selection?

When an organism has an inherited trait that gives it an advantage in a particular environment, natural selection can begin to work. That organism will probably survive longer and produce more offspring than others of its species. As a result, the species will change gradually as more of its members have the helpful trait.

Natural selection explains why many species have coloring that helps them to blend in with their environment. Individuals with markings that stand out are easy targets for predators, and thus, have less chance to reproduce. Well-hidden creatures have more opportunity to mate and pass their camouflage genes to future generations.

▲ Dark
peppered moth

▲ Normal peppered moth

Albino trout are easy targets

A large number of trout and salmon born in artificial breeding farms are albino, yet it is nearly impossible to find an albino trout or salmon in the wild. Normal rainbow trout are striped and spotted with various shades of brown and yellow. To a heron or kingfisher, these colors look much like the bottom of a stream, making it difficult for the bird to spot the fish *(below)*. Albino fish, which are white, are easy for the waterfowl to spot and rarely survive long enough to produce offspring.

▼ Albino trout

● Pollution and natural selection

In the 1800s pollution in English cities enabled natural selection to operate on a group of peppered moths. When industrialization began, most peppered moths were pale with black splotches *(near left)*, which gave them the appearance of lichen on tree bark, hiding them from predators. Only a few moths were dark *(far left)*. Soon, soot from factories turned city trees and buildings dark brown, and pale moths became visible to birds. Within a few years, the dark moth became common in cities, although the speckled form prevailed in the cleaner countryside.

Do Breeding and Evolution Differ?

Nature has the guiding hand in evolution, weeding out mutations that hinder an organism's ability to survive in the wild. Humans, though, have learned to use mutations to produce plants and animals that serve some useful or desired purpose. This is called breeding, or artificial selection. In many cases, these mutations produce an organism unfit for survival in the natural world. But these creations thrive under the protective care of humans, so the mutations persist.

The domestic chicken is a good example. Its ancestor, which lives in Asian jungles, is a wily creature that lays perhaps a dozen eggs a year. In contrast, today's chickens, some of which produce a dozen eggs a month, would quickly become extinct if released into the wild.

Fancy goldfish from plain carp

There are more than 125 breeds of goldfish, from the common pet-shop variety to exotic breeds with protruding eyes, missing fins, hooded heads, and wild colors *(right)*. Yet all descend from the wild goldfish *(below)*, a greenish brown member of the carp family. The Chinese bred the first goldfish nearly 1,000 years ago.

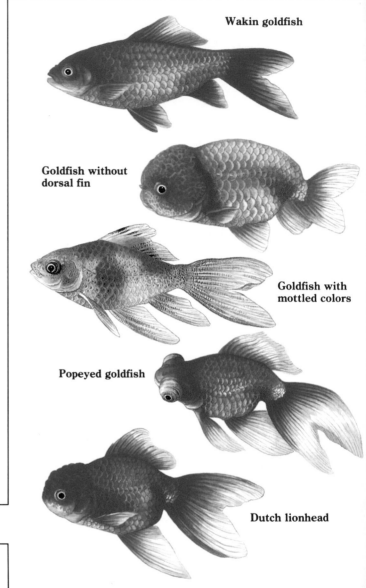

Wakin goldfish

Goldfish without dorsal fin

Goldfish with mottled colors

Popeyed goldfish

Dutch lionhead

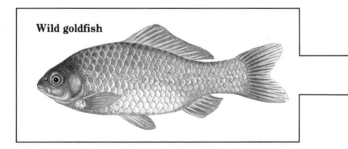

Wild goldfish

A red mutation

A mutation in the wild goldfish produces offspring with red color. These served as the forebears of today's goldfish. Even after hundreds of years of breeding, some goldfish must still possess normal coloration genes—when released into the wild, goldfish regain their ancient carp colors within several generations.

Wild goldfish

Red goldfish

Pedigreed cats

The Egyptians began breeding cats some 3,500 years ago, and today there are about 30 distinct breeds of cats. Little is known about the ancestry of modern cats. Some breeds, particularly tabbies, probably descended from the Libyan wildcat, which still lives in Africa.

Manx cat

Siamese cat

Himalayan

Persian cat

Chartreux

Libyan wildcat

Dozens of cabbages

Broccoli, cauliflower, Brussels sprouts, and the 100 or so other types of cabbage grown today all arose from the wild cabbage, which still grows on the mountainous shores of the Mediterranean. By selecting for particular traits, breeders have produced scores of plants that enrich the human diet.

Cabbage

Cauliflower

Ornamental kale

Brussels sprouts

Kohlrabi

Broccoli

Wild cabbage

Crossbreeding

Producing a new breed does not always require waiting for a chance mutation to occur. Often, breeders will mate two breeds to produce a new, third breed. The Himalayan breed of cat arose from repeated matings between Persian and Siamese cats. The new breed has characteristics of both its ancestors.

Siamese cat

Persian cat

Himalayan cat

What Is Adaptation?

Adaptation is often the end result of natural selection. Each species is fitted in some way to the characteristics of its environment and, in this manner, fills a niche in the planet's ecology. If the environment changes, those adaptations may no longer help the species. When such changes occur slowly, natural selection may operate and the species may evolve new adaptations. But rapid environmental changes can doom the species to extinction before adaptation can take place.

Some scientists believe that dinosaurs became extinct for this reason: The Earth's climate changed, and these large reptiles were unable to adapt to the new conditions. Mammals, small and with a faster birthrate, were better adapted to the new seasons.

The Arctic fox, with its white winter fur and small ears, is well adapted to life in the tundra. Its paw pads are covered with fur so that it can walk easily in snow.

The red fox lives across Europe and North America. It has moderate-size ears, and its coat retains its red color all year.

Adaptation in foxes

A mammal's ears do more than just collect sound—they also act as a radiator to give off excess heat. Fox species live in all types of climates, and their ears reflect the local temperatures. At the extremes are the Arctic fox, with its small, heat-conserving ears, and the fennec, a desert dweller with ears as large as its skull.

Fennecs are small foxes that live in the Sahara. Their coats are sand-colored, enabling them to blend into their background and sneak up on prey. A fennec can go for days without drinking. Like the Arctic fox, the fennec has fur-covered paw pads, allowing it to walk easily on sand.

Adaptation in cacti

The ancestors of modern cacti lived in tropical jungles. As the species spread to other, drier regions, they evolved with new traits that helped them survive with less water. Stems grew, for example, becoming water reservoirs and taking on the task of photosynthesis. This enabled the leaves to shrink, becoming protective needles.

Alpine cacti. Long, white, hairlike spines reflect the intense ultraviolet light present in Alpine regions. The body of an Alpine cactus can expand to absorb and store occasional rainfall.

Desert cacti. The folds in a desert cactus allow it to swell and absorb tremendous amounts of water. The needles block water-stealing air currents from rushing past the plant's body.

Tropical relatives. To this day, relatives of cactus species live in moist tropical jungles. They have more in common with other tropical plants than with cacti living in desert and Alpine regions.

How Do Species Differentiate?

One mark of a species is that all its members can interbreed. They also have a specific pattern of physical traits and behaviors. Variations exist in some of a species' features, but the differences within a species are far smaller than those found between two species.

The basis for both the sameness and variation lies in a species' genes. Since members of a species can mate freely with each other, a species' genes are constantly reshuffled with each generation. Thus any variations will be spread evenly throughout a species, and the species does not change. But if a barrier separates some members of a species from the larger group, certain variations can become more common in the isolated population, and evolution may occur. Over time, the isolated group may differ enough from the parent group that members of the two groups cannot mate even if the barrier disappears.

Butterflies can easily cross over a small but growing ridge. The ridge is not an effective barrier, so members of the species can mix freely.

Geographic isolation

Geographic isolation has played an important role in the evolution of species. The Earth's surface has changed much since life first appeared. Volcanoes erupted from the seafloor, creating land where none existed. Mountain chains thrust upward. Oceans rose, separating peninsulas from mainlands. Perhaps the greatest rift occurred hundreds of millions of years ago, when the supercontinent Pangaea split up, gradually moving today's continents apart and creating the oceans. Most differentiation occurs slowly, matching the rate of most geographic changes.

Today, human activity produces geographic isolation quickly. Differentiation occurred in some Central American bird and insect species after the Panama Canal was built. Similarly, two groups of animals can be cut off from each other after logging operations open large holes in the forest cover.

Over time the ridge grows into a mountain range, and the separated groups evolve into two distinct species.

Erosion produces a gap in the mountains, letting the butterfly populations mix. Unable to mate successfully with each other, however, they remain distinct species. If they do not vie for the same resources, both may survive in this area.

Wild goldfish live on the bottom of freshwater lakes, eating roots and insects. They have short intestines and few gill rakers, which filter food from water.

Ecological isolation

Some variations within a species may allow an individual to move into a new ecological niche by taking advantage of conditions that differ slightly from those of its home territory. In this way, a new species may form while the original continues to exist. In one lake, for example, a species of goldfish that feeds on plankton evolved from ancestors that could only eat roots and insects on the lake's bottom *(below)*.

Some wild goldfish had longer intestines and many gill rakers, and could filter plankton from water. They began living closer to the surface, where plankton are found.

The surface dwellers became flatter and developed larger mouths. This let them suck more water into their mouths and collect more plankton.

M.K

23

What Is Macroevolution?

At certain times in the course of evolution, the many small changes that produce new species accumulate to the point where, suddenly, a radically different form of life appears. From that one species, many new species evolve—the tree of life grows a new large branch from which dozens of smaller branches will develop. This dramatic change is known as macroevolution, or adaptive radiation. An example is when the first feathered reptile appeared; this was the ancestor of all the birds that have evolved since.

In the animal kingdom, an early macroevolution produced an eel-like species with a spinal cord but no backbone. The next huge step occurred when the first fish evolved, with its weight-supporting backbone. The appearance of lobe-finned fish, which were able to breathe on land, represents another macroevolution. Millions of years later, the first reptile appeared, and millions of years after that, the first mammal.

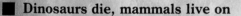

The last dinosaurs became extinct at the end of the Mesozoic era, 65 million years ago.

■ **Dinosaurs die, mammals live on**

Dinosaurs had dominated the planet for some 150 million years when suddenly, about 65 million years ago, they became extinct *(above and right)*. In fact, up to 50 percent of all genuses alive at the time died off, including most of the reptiles. There are many theories that attempt to explain this mass extinction. One theory holds that a huge asteroid slammed into the Earth, creating a giant dust cloud that blocked out the sun's energy and caused plants, a major food source, to die. Another theory says that continental drift caused the seasons to change, and the dinosaurs could not adjust. Regardless of why it occurred, the dinosaurs' death was a break for the smaller mammals that were clinging to existence then. Without competition from the dinosaurs, mammals experienced a tremendous burst of evolution as they quickly moved into many of the habitats once held by the dinosaurs *(far right)*.

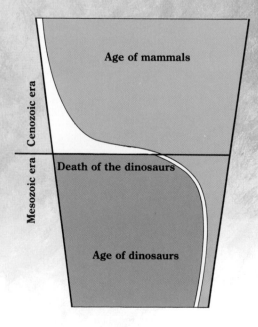

Cenozoic era

Mesozoic era

Age of mammals

Death of the dinosaurs

Age of dinosaurs

Opening a new world

As competition on land grew fierce, some creatures took to the sky and adapted to that life. Eventually, flying predators also appeared, and life in the air became as complex as life on the ground and underwater.

Mammals thrived in the new world left vacant by the dinosaurs' demise. Evolution produced all manner of mammals.

2
Where Life Began

The history of planet Earth began about 4.6 billion years ago, and the beginning of life on Earth dates back almost as far. Scientists know this because they have found fossils from what is called the Precambrian era, which covers the time until the Cambrian period. These fossils represent small, humble life forms. While fossils from the Cambrian period, 500 million to 570 million years ago, tell the story of life as seen in the first hard-shell animals, Precambrian creatures did not have hard structures, and their fossils can only hint about life long ago.

Precambrian fossils known as stromatolites are moundlike structures with dark and light bands. But within the dark bands, scientists have found traces of tiny one-celled organisms that lived at least 3.5 billion years ago. These organisms, which resemble modern bacteria called blue-green algae, or cyanobacteria, were the first to use the sun's energy to convert water and dissolved carbon dioxide into food. This process, called photosynthesis, releases oxygen as a by-product. By adding oxygen to an atmosphere that previously had almost none, these organisms set the stage for the evolution of all creatures that depend on oxygen to live.

Just before animals with shells evolved, the first organisms with more than one cell appeared. Their soft bodies left only faint impressions in the mud of the seas where they lived, but scientists speculate that many of them are related to creatures living today.

Mats of blue-green algae and sediment release oxygen into the Precambrian atmosphere *(above)*. Below, the path of evolution leading to modern mammals.

How Did the Earth Form?

The Earth grew from a cloud of gases and dust swirling around the newly formed Sun. Particles in the cloud, pulled together by gravity, condensed into a rocky ball that continued to attract bits of rock and dust into its orbit. This constant shower of fiery meteors added mass to the growing planet. And as the Earth grew larger, its gravity increased, squeezing its core and boosting the internal temperature of the young planet. More shrinking and heating sent molten rock flowing across the surface of the Earth. Gases bubbled out of the rising lava and escaped to form a primitive atmosphere that trapped heat near the sizzling planet.

The steaming Earth forms oceans

Gases escaping from molten lava flowing from the Earth's interior set free many chemicals trapped inside the planet. One of those substances—the one upon which all life depends—was water. Escaping as vapor, or steam, at the planet's red-hot surface, the water condensed in the black cold of space and rained back down, only to turn into steam again when it hit Earth's surface. This went on until the maturing Earth began to cool; then some water remained on the surface, running downhill to pool in craters created by striking meteors. By the end of its first billion years, the Earth had oceans, salted with minerals dissolved out of the crust and simmering with continuing volcanic activity. These early oceans nurtured the chemicals that would later combine to begin the evolution of life.

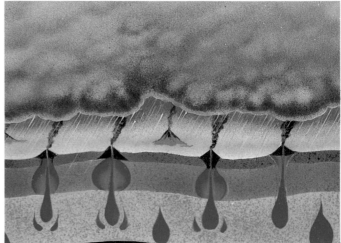

In the Earth's shrinking interior, radioactive substances decayed, helping to melt rock. Lava released gases to form an early atmosphere and water that vaporized and rained back down on Earth.

As the Earth matured and its surface cooled, rain no longer vaporized when it hit the crust. First tiny rivulets formed, then rivers, dissolving minerals out of the surface rocks and forming great pools.

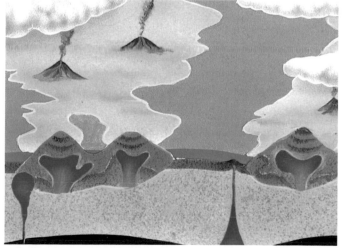

Further cooling caused the Earth's crust to break into huge plates. Surface water collected in the depressions, forming oceans. Once-abundant gases, such as carbon dioxide, began to be absorbed into the oceans and rock.

How Did Life Originate?

The young Earth seemed an unlikely place for life to begin. Volcanoes splattered red-hot lava over the gray rocky crust, and the sun's searing ultraviolet light scorched the surface. Lightning split the cloudy sky, and the harsh chemicals of the early atmosphere, such as carbon monoxide, would have poisoned almost any organism living today. But scientists speculate that energy from lightning, sunlight, and volcanic eruptions eventually linked some of the atoms in the atmosphere into simple organic molecules. And these molecules—which form the basic building blocks of the chemicals of life—then rained onto the Earth's surface and into its warm, salty oceans. There, the molecules—called amino acids—formed chains of proteins, which in turn linked up into the vital nucleic acids DNA and RNA.

Amino acid

Protein

The watery cradle of life

When the molecule-rich rain hit the Earth, it ran over the surface rocks, collecting minerals on its way to the oceans. The seas were soon a nourishing soup, stirring together the chemicals necessary for life. Amino acids linked up into long chains called proteins. Phosphate molecules, sugars, and organic bases combined to form nucleotides. And nucleotides in turn formed the nucleic acids DNA and RNA.

In modern cells, DNA holds an organism's genetic information, RNA sends the information to the proteins, and the proteins start the chemical reactions necessary to carry out the instructions. Some scientists believe RNA may have been the first chemical to form, since it can both hold genetic instructions and, like a protein, carry them out. In this scenario, DNA and protein would have evolved later.

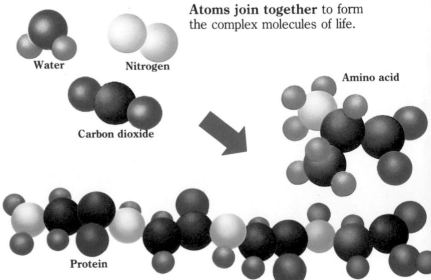

Atoms join together to form the complex molecules of life.

Water

Nitrogen

Carbon dioxide

Amino acid

Protein

H₂O

N₂

CO₂

Amino acid

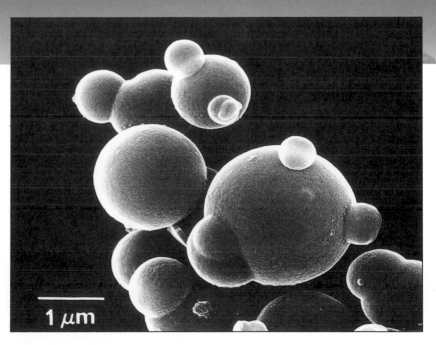

1 μm

Chemicals of life in the laboratory

In 1953 a chemist named Stanley M. Miller attempted to re-create the conditions of the young Earth in the laboratory. He filled a glass flask with a warm "ocean" and an "atmosphere" composed of methane, ammonia, and hydrogen gases. He sent strong sparks through the gases to imitate lightning. After only a day, Miller could detect amino acids in his miniature ocean. Later, other experiments showed that these amino acids could combine to form proteins. Under the right conditions, the proteins would even form microscopic hollow balls *(right)*. These spheres—some of which look surprisingly like bacteria—grow by absorbing material from their surroundings. When they reach a certain size, buds develop, then split off. Such tiny protein spheres might have been the first ancestors of living cells.

What Were the First Living Things?

The first living things on Earth were simple cells, probably consisting of nucleic acids and proteins surrounded by a thin cell membrane. These cells must have been far simpler than most modern bacteria. None of them could use sunlight to make food the way plants and some bacteria do today, and they lived in a very different environment. The air contained almost no oxygen, and the ocean water was very warm.

Although these simple cells lived billions of years ago, scientists today have found similar organisms living at the bottom of the ocean. At spots more than a mile deep, where molten rock sits just below the seafloor, hot water blasts upward from the Earth's interior. These jets of water—called black smokers—carry a heavy load of gases and minerals that turn the water black. While most of the deep ocean floor is with-

1

out any kind of life, black smokers form the centers of busy communities. Bacteria thrive here without oxygen or light, getting their energy from hydrogen sulfide and other compounds forced upward by the hot water. Some scientists studying black smokers and the similarities between these modern-day bacteria and the Earth's first simple cells suggest that life may have begun around these hot water vents.

The simplest modern-day cells

Of all life on Earth, bacteria are among the simplest—small cells with no specialized compartments inside. And the anaerobic bacteria living around black smokers may be the most primitive. Some scientists believe these organisms—called archaebacteria, or ancient bacteria—are direct descendants of the ancestors of all living things. Others say the bacteria evolved long after other life forms and adapted to such harsh environments as sewage, hot springs, and the intestines of some animals. Ancient bacteria thrive today, for instance, in the boiling springs found in Yellowstone National Park *(above)*.

1. Bacteria living near black smokers process gases and minerals to grow. The energy they release as a by-product helps provide food for football-size clams, giant tubeworms, and other organisms in the deep-sea community.

2

2. Black smokers form when water seeps into cracks in the seafloor and meets molten rock just below the surface. The water is superheated and surges upward, carrying with it dissolved minerals. When the scalding water meets the cold seawater above the ocean floor, some of the minerals solidify and form tall chimneys. Others collect into particles—the black "smoke" that gives the vents their name—and spray out of the chimneys. Pressure keeps the water from boiling, allowing it to reach 600° to 650° F. Scientists think black smokers have existed since continents first began to drift apart.

What Added Oxygen to the Air?

When the first living things appeared on Earth, there may have been little or no oxygen in the air. Then blue-green algae, also known as cyanobacteria, evolved. Blue-greens, as they are called, used the sun's energy to turn water and dissolved carbon dioxide into food. This process, called aerobic photosynthesis, released oxygen into the atmosphere, allowing oxygen-consuming cells to develop.

In the ocean, blue-greens sometimes form stromatolites, mounds of layered sediment and cyanobacteria. Fossil stromatolites at least 3.5 billion years old have been discovered.

Sediment and fossilized cells form a stromatolite.

How a stromatolite forms

Scientists studying living stromatolites have found that blue-greens grow in a row of cells joined together in a chain. During the day the cells grow and divide and the chain lengthens. At night growth stops. Waves constantly wash over the blue-greens, separating the chains and depositing particles of sediment between them and on top of them. The next day, the blue-greens again seek the light, growing upward through the sediment and adding new cells. The cells produce calcium carbonate, a kind of cement that glues the layers together. Alternating periods of growth and rest eventually build lumpy, hardened structures called stromatolites.

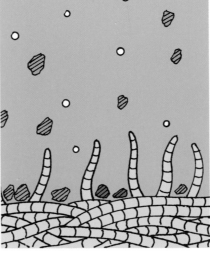

Sticky tendrils trap sediment between the chains of growing blue-green algae.

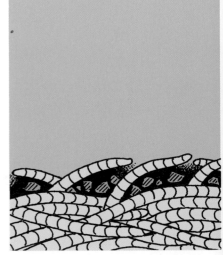

Blue-green cells secrete calcium carbonate—what many seashells are made of—to seal the layers.

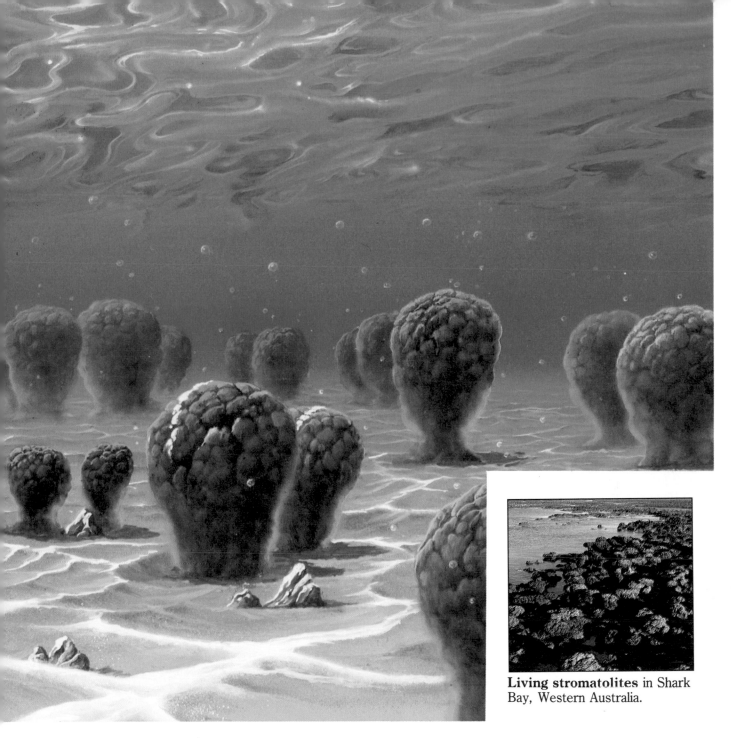

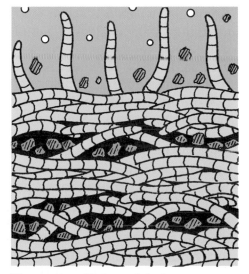

Living stromatolites in Shark Bay, Western Australia.

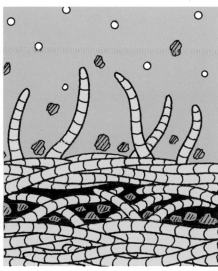

As daylight returns tendrils of blue-greens grow, pushing their way up through the sand.

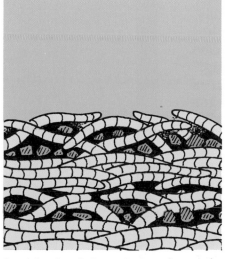

At night the chains stop growing, and a new layer of sediment gradually builds up on top of them.

The cycles of light and dark, growth and rest, eventually create a layered stromatolite.

How Did Cells Evolve?

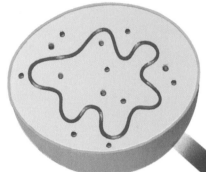

Early simple cells likely consisted of proteins *(red dots)* and RNA *(thin purple loop)* surrounded by a thin cell membrane.

A new nucleic acid, DNA *(purple loop),* appeared later, creating cells similar to those of modern bacteria.

Chloroplasts may have appeared when large simple cells took over smaller ones capable of aerobic photosynthesis.

Mitochondria probably evolved when prokaryotes took over smaller cells that used oxygen to produce energy.

All cells are either complex or simple. A complex cell has a nucleus that contains DNA, a nucleic acid that stores genetic information. Animals, plants, fungi, and some single-celled organisms have complex cells, which are called eukaryotes, meaning "true nucleus." Simple cells, which make up bacteria and blue-greens, have no nucleus; they are called prokaryotes, meaning "before nucleus."

Complex cells contain structures called mitochondria, which use oxygen to produce energy for the cell. In addition, the cells of plants and some single-celled organisms contain chloroplasts, where photosynthesis takes place. Mitochondria and chloroplasts may have developed when large simple cells ingested smaller ones. Over millions of years, the two structures became specialized. They cannot live on their own but contain DNA and can reproduce.

A variety of bacteria inhabit almost every environment on Earth. All bacteria are prokaryotes, with no nucleus.

Simple blue-green algae, or blue-greens, contain a kind of chlorophyll, the chemical machinery of photosynthesis.

Plant cells have rigid walls outside the cell membrane. Inside they have a nucleus, mitochondria, and chloroplasts.

Soft-sided animal cells contain a nucleus, mitochondria, and a number of other specialized cell structures.

Some simple bacteria get their energy from chemicals. Found in extreme environments, they may be similar to the earliest cells.

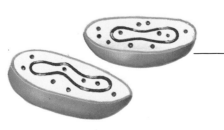

How Did Multicelled Life Evolve?

The first organisms probably were made up of single, simple cells. Yet today many organisms have millions of specialized cells working together. No one knows exactly how multicelled organisms evolved. Scientists suggest that single-celled eukaryotes may have formed colonies of identical cells, which then became specialized. Another theory says that the complex single-celled eukaryotes evolved internal cell membranes that divided the original cell into many specialized cells. Clues as to what these first multicelled eukaryotes were like—and how closely they resemble modern creatures—can be found today in fossils.

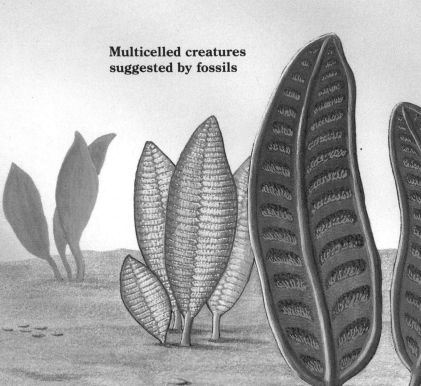

Multicelled creatures suggested by fossils

Fossils reveal the imprints, tracks, and burrows of segmented worms that are possibly related to earthworms that exist today.

Some fossils suggest animals like today's sea pens, which in reality are colonies of small, multicelled animals.

A colony of similar cells

Using certain modern single-celled eukaryotes as models, scientists have developed a theory of how multicelled eukaryotes may have evolved. These organisms, called flagellates, move or draw food toward the cell with long whiplike structures called flagella. Some flagellates occur in colonies of four or more identical cells. In larger colonies, some cells may be specialized. Sponges, the simplest multicelled organisms, have many flagellate feeding cells and other specialized cell types. Though sponges do not appear to be the ancestors of any modern organisms, a gradual process of increasing cell numbers and specialization could have allowed colonies to evolve into true multicelled organisms.

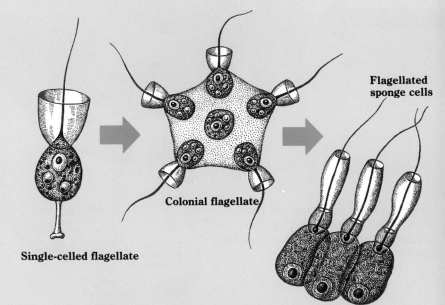

Flagellated sponge cells

Colonial flagellate

Single-celled flagellate

Animals resembling jellyfish left their mark in the fossil record—faint imprints in fine sand or mud that later hardened into rocky fossils.

◄ This segmented wormlike animal called *Spriggina* may have given rise to trilobites, once-abundant organisms that are now extinct.

Fossils suggest that a bowl-shaped organism lived at the bottom of the sea, but scientists don't yet know what it may be related to.

Dickinsonia, a rounded, segmented, wormlike animal about 2½ inches long, may be a relative of modern-day segmented worms.

A complex single cell subdivides

Some scientists have proposed an alternative to the widely accepted colony theory of how multicelled organisms arose. Some modern single-celled organisms, such as paramecia, have very complex internal structures, including a mouthlike gullet, openings that hold and digest food, and openings that contract to expel excess water. The paramecium and its relatives are sometimes called acellular, meaning "without cells," instead of single-celled. Acellular organisms could have developed internal divisions—like cell membranes—that divided one cell into many. A modern multicelled animal called an acoel flatworm has been proposed as the descendant of organisms like the paramecium.

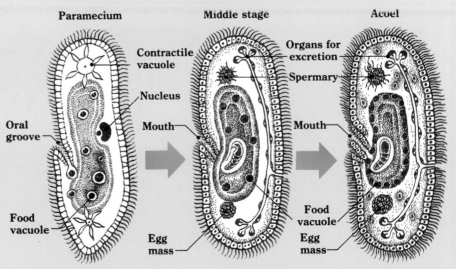

Paramecium — Middle stage — Acoel

Contractile vacuole

Nucleus

Oral groove

Mouth

Food vacuole

Egg mass

Organs for excretion

Spermary

Mouth

Food vacuole

Egg mass

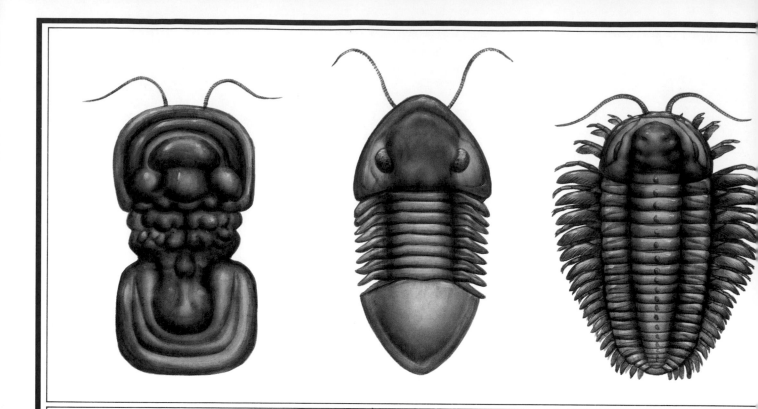

3

The Paleozoic: Dawn of Modern Life

The Paleozoic era was a time of great change in Earth's life history. During the era's 325-million-year span, the early mold for every modern life form, from ferns to humans, was cast.

During the Cambrian period, beginning 570 million years ago, soft-bodied invertebrates—animals without backbones—branched out into more than 1,200 species of shelled creatures, including the scrappy bottom-feeders trilobites *(above)*. By the late Cambrian, the planet saw the rise of the first vertebrates—jawless fish with armored heads. By the early Silurian, these pre-

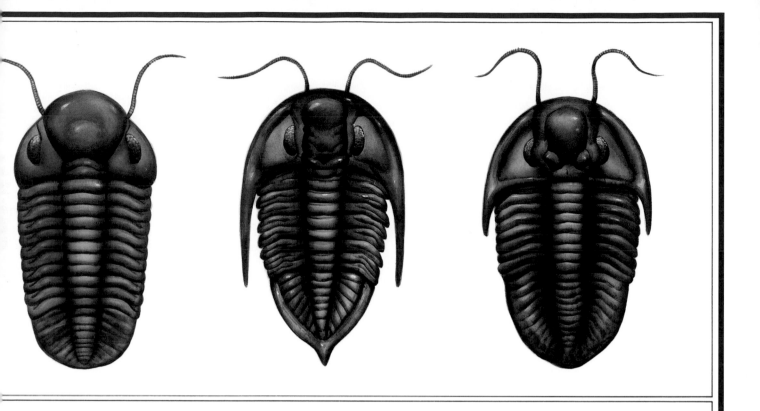

historic swimmers were joined by jawed fish, while on land, plants had begun to sprout.

The course of evolutionary change broadened during the Devonian period when animals—spiders and primitive insects—took up life on land. At the same time, lobe-finned fish migrated into muddy inland rivers and swamps, where, living half in and half out of the water, they evolved into amphibians, the first land vertebrates.

The final periods of the Paleozoic were a time of extraordinary change. Around 345 million years ago, the warm climate of the Carboniferous period turned marshlands into forests of towering tree ferns. Enormous dragonflies and six-foot-long worms lived in these jungles, providing tasty fare for amphibians and their descendants, the reptiles. The rise of reptiles during the Permian period was among the last major events of the Paleozoic era. This chapter will explore the forces that led to their creation.

An evolutionary milestone marks each of the Paleozoic's six periods, beginning with shelled marine animals in the Cambrian and ending with reptiles in the Permian.

What Lived 500 Million Years Ago?

In 1909, while scouting the Canadian Rockies, the American paleontologist Charles Doolittle Walcott stumbled upon the fossilized remains of 530-million-year-old creatures. During Cambrian times, they had lived on a muddy shelf in the shallow seas of North America. An underwater mud slide had dislodged the ledge dwellers, dumping them into the cold, oxygenless depths below. There they were preserved in perfect detail in the sediment. Over the millennia, that sediment compacted to form what is now known as the Burgess Shale.

Unlike Precambrian fossil beds, which showed unidentifiable creatures, the Burgess Shale contained a startling variety of well-defined life forms. Its rich diversity included many soft-

Sea lily

Marrella

Brachiopod

Sanctacaris

Trilobite

Cephalopod

Rugose coral

Hallucigenia

bodied creatures that are usually lost to the fossil record, including many animals that proved to be evolutionary dead ends—a host of bizarre creatures never seen before or since.

The Burgess Shale gave paleontologists a glimpse into a great explosion of life on Earth. Though many animals thrived in the Precambrian era, it was not until the Cambrian period—when warm seas had eroded the continental rock into mountains of nutrient-rich, sheltering muds—that conditions favored rapid evolution. Into this vast field of opportunity radiated a marvelous wealth of hard-bodied life forms, each a daring experiment in survival. Some of these creatures, along with other remarkable life forms of the early Paleozoic era, are shown here.

Sea lily. The most numerous and successful of its crinoid class, this flowerlike echinoderm was armored with limy scales and held fast to the bottom by its stalk.

Marrella. Breathing through feathery gills on its legs, this tiny arthropod, which is also known as the lace crab, thrived during the Cambrian period.

Sanctacaris. Like modern-day chelicerates, this arthropod was a strong swimmer and a predator specialized for direct pursuit.

Brachiopod. This brachiopod's soft body was covered by a hinged lime shell, out of which extended a flexible stalk for anchoring to the mud.

Trilobite. Among the most abundant arthropods of the Cambrian period, bottom-feeding trilobites averaged 2 to 3 inches in length.

Nautiloid cephalopod. This mollusk captured prey with its tentacles.

Rugose coral. The tentacles of this ancient coelenterate looked like those of a sea anemone. A calcite cone supported its soft body.

Hallucigenia. Skittering about on seven pairs of knitting-needle legs, this fantastic creature also had seven mouths, one at the end of each waving tentacle.

Pirania. These many-celled animals, similar to today's sponges, secreted skeletons covered with sharp spicules.

Mackenzia. Paleontologists consider this creature to be a sea anemone.

Slit shell. This snail produced a swirling shell with a bottom slit expelling water.

Blastozoan. Exterior plates protected the soft tissues of this echinoderm, whose tendril-like appendages swept food into its waiting mouth.

Honeycomb coral. The soft-bodied polyps of these coelenterates formed large reefs in the Paleozoic era.

Archaeocyathids. Once thought to be the evolutionary link between sponges and corals, these "ancient cups" formed the first reeflike deposits of the Paleozoic era.

What Were Trilobites Like?

Paleozoic seas were filled with trilobites, armored arthropods whose outer coverings, or cuticles, became many of the finest fossils of their age. Like lobsters, trilobites had to shed their horny casings in order to grow; these collected in great piles on the seafloor.

From fossil tracks, paleontologists know that most trilobites swept along the ocean bottom seeking food. A few paddled through the seas, using their oarlike legs. Depending on their feeding habits and the depth of their ocean home, trilobites evolved different kinds of eyes. Those living in murky waters had tiny, sightless orbs or no eyes at all. Others had wide-angle eyes with 15,000 lenses for extrasharp vision.

Sea scorpion

Trilobite life stages

A newly hatched trilobite, or protaspid, was little more than a head and tail within a one-piece shell. As a meraspid, it added segments to form a midsection, gradually growing into an adult holaspid.

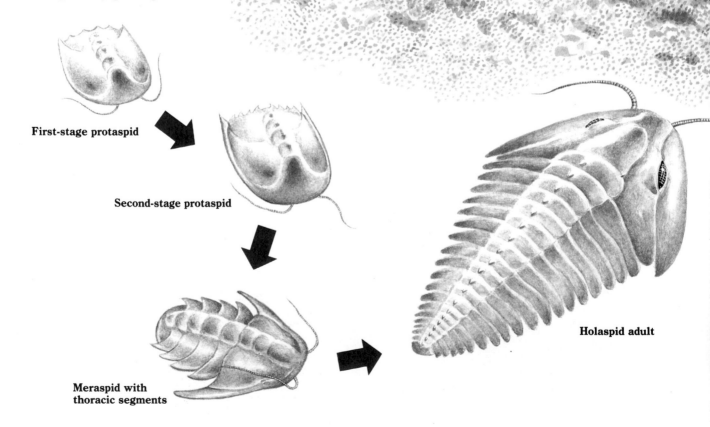

First-stage protaspid

Second-stage protaspid

Meraspid with thoracic segments

Holaspid adult

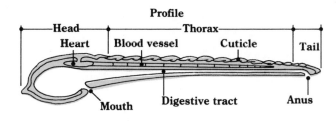

A threatened trilobite rolls to avoid capture.

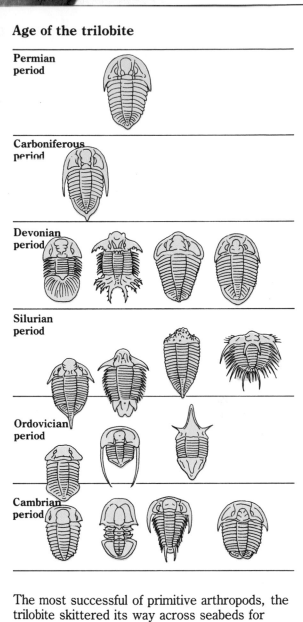

Age of the trilobite

Permian period

Carboniferous period

Devonian period

Silurian period

Ordovician period

Cambrian period

The most successful of primitive arthropods, the trilobite skittered its way across seabeds for more than 300 million years. Trilobite populations peaked during the Cambrian period, then declined to extinction by the end of the Paleozoic era.

Trilobite anatomy

Trilobites, or "three-lobed ones," take their name from the three lengthwise sections that ran from the head through the thorax and into the tail. A molded plate protected both head and tail; nested between were the flexible, muscled segments of the thorax, which, in primitive species, numbered as many as 40. From each segment sprouted a pair of jointed legs with gills for breathing.

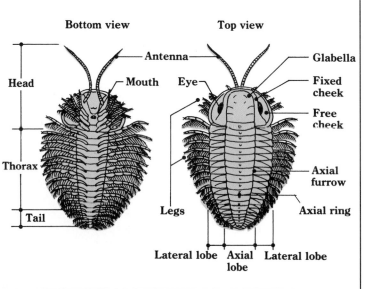

Profile

Head — Thorax — Tail
Heart — Blood vessel — Cuticle
Mouth — Digestive tract — Anus

Bottom view

Head — Antenna — Mouth
Thorax
Tail — Legs

Top view

Antenna — Glabella
Eye — Fixed cheek
Free cheek
Axial furrow
Axial ring
Lateral lobe — Axial lobe — Lateral lobe

How Did Backboned Animals Evolve?

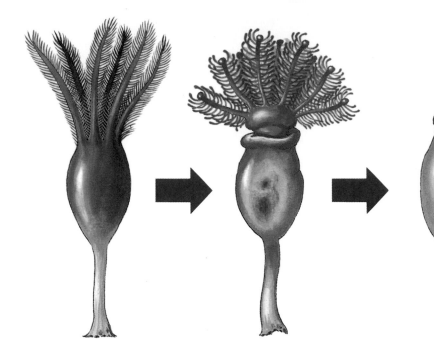

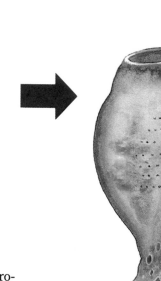

A urochordate adult

The ancestor of all backboned animals, or vertebrates, may have been a saclike echinoderm with feeding arms that were similar to those of the sea lily.

Over time, the echinoderm ancestor may have evolved into a hemichordate—an elaborately branched marine creature, known as a pterobranch, that lived inside a fleshy cup. It drew in food by beating the feathery cilia on its branches.

Eventually, the pterobranch evolved gill slits. These allowed the creature to hide in its body cup while taking food from the water. Later, the animal evolved into a urochordate *(right)* like the sea squirt.

● **A jawless mouth**

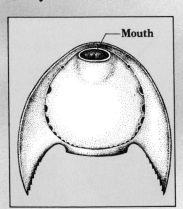

Mouth

▲ **Like all** agnathans, *Kiaeraspis*—shown here from the underside—had no jaw and so could use its mouth only to suck.

Jamoytius kerwoodie had an internal cartilage basket supporting its gills, like modern lampreys. It lived at the end of the Silurian period.

A freshwater fish of the Devonian period, *Hemicyclaspis* skimmed the bottom for algae and other organic matter in the mud.

Among the curious Paleozoic creatures that were preserved in the Burgess Shale was a 3-inch-long swimmer whose wormlike form showed the traces of a stiffened rod, or notochord. Named *Pikaia,* the delicate animal was the earliest known chordate—the forerunner of all life forms that have a stiff back support.

Surprisingly, scientists believe that *Pikaia* and, in fact, all chordates, including humans, descended from an echinoderm, as shown at left.

Though these creatures do not look much like chordates, one species, the bottle-shaped sea squirt, spawns free-swimming larvae that have notochords and gills—as do all vertebrate embryos (developing young). Some of these sea squirt larvae might have reproduced before turning into adults, generating offspring with vertebrate characteristics. Such "halfway" creatures are considered the ancestors of the first vertebrate fish, the agnathans.

A urochordate larva

The urochordate's larva had the gill slits of its parent, a rod of cartilage known as the notochord, and a hollow dorsal nerve cord. The last two features may have vanished as it grew.

By keeping some larval characteristics when grown, some urochordates may have produced offspring with the notochords and gills of their parents.

■ **The first vertebrates**

Saw-nosed *Doryaspis* had a head shield flattened for gliding through the water.

Drepanaspis was a bottom-feeder of the early Devonian period. Its mouth was surrounded by a bony shield.

The Devonian fish *Pteraspis* sported an armored suit and razor fins.

Thelodus first appeared in the Silurian period. Its body was covered with tiny scales.

How Did Jaws Develop?

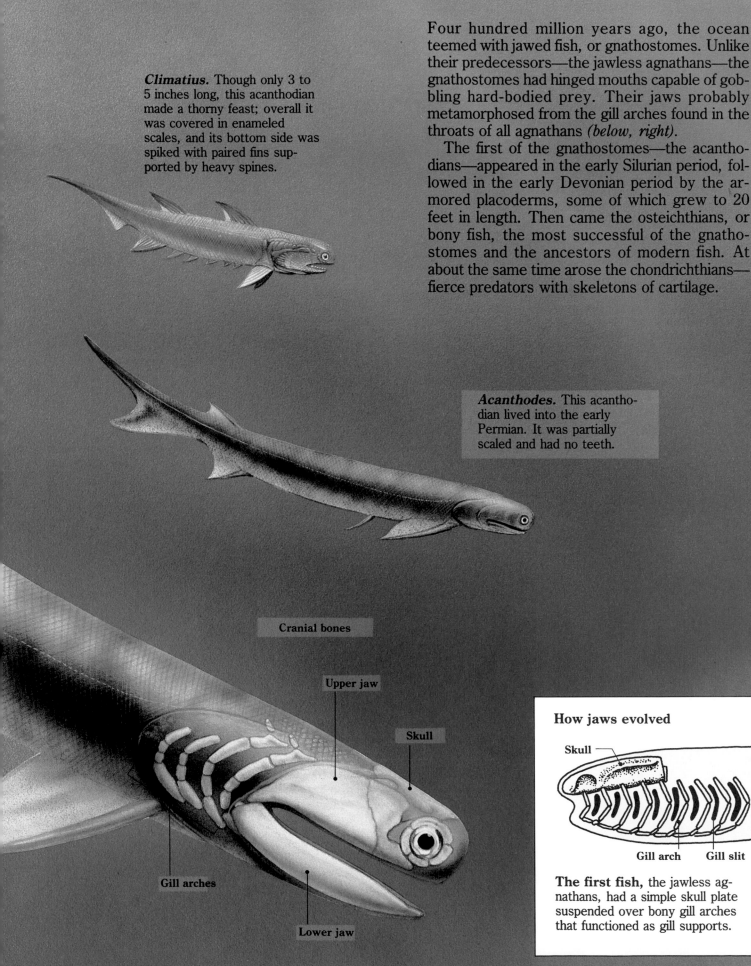

Climatius. Though only 3 to 5 inches long, this acanthodian made a thorny feast; overall it was covered in enameled scales, and its bottom side was spiked with paired fins supported by heavy spines.

Four hundred million years ago, the ocean teemed with jawed fish, or gnathostomes. Unlike their predecessors—the jawless agnathans—the gnathostomes had hinged mouths capable of gobbling hard-bodied prey. Their jaws probably metamorphosed from the gill arches found in the throats of all agnathans *(below, right)*.

The first of the gnathostomes—the acanthodians—appeared in the early Silurian period, followed in the early Devonian period by the armored placoderms, some of which grew to 20 feet in length. Then came the osteichthians, or bony fish, the most successful of the gnathostomes and the ancestors of modern fish. At about the same time arose the chondrichthians—fierce predators with skeletons of cartilage.

Acanthodes. This acanthodian lived into the early Permian. It was partially scaled and had no teeth.

Cranial bones

Upper jaw

Skull

Gill arches

Lower jaw

How jaws evolved

Skull

Gill arch   Gill slit

The first fish, the jawless agnathans, had a simple skull plate suspended over bony gill arches that functioned as gill supports.

Cheirolepis. The sturgeon may be a descendant of *Cheirolepis,* an osteichthian whose 19-inch body wore a coat of small scales.

▼ **Dunkleosteus.** A true monster of the deep, this 20-foot-long placoderm probably lurked on the bottom, waiting for prey.

Coccosteus. A hinge between the head and trunk of this placoderm allowed it to open its mouth wide.

Cladoselache. A primitive shark, *Cladoselache* was a fast-swimming chondrichthian that measured some 4 feet in length and had a powerful jaw.

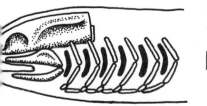

Over time, the first two gill arches disappeared and the third collapsed and swung forward to enclose the mouth, forming upper and lower jawbones.

Spiracle

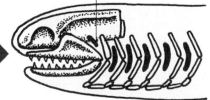

Bones studded with teeth fused to the jawbones, while the fourth gill arch shifted forward to support the jaw. Its gill slit formed a spiracle.

One widely accepted theory of jaw evolution proposes that jaws developed from the arches bracing the gills inside the mouths of primitive agnathans *(far left).* Fossils of the first jawed fish—the spiny acanthodians—dating from the Silurian period show that early jawbones were thin and weakly fused to the skull *(middle).* By the Devonian period, however, when the first chondrichthians and osteichthians appeared, stronger links between the lengthened jawbones and skull made for a scissorlike bite *(near left).*

What Were the First Land Creatures?

Not long after land plants appeared, about 420 million years ago, animals ventured out of the sea to feast on them and shelter in their moist underbrush. The earliest fossil is of a millipede, a many-legged arthropod of the class Myriapoda that favored the litter of land plants. Over the next 15 million years other classes of arthropods arrived—spiders and mites (class Arachnida) and wingless collembolans (class Hexapoda). Lured by such prey, predators such as centipedes soon colonized the fringes of the land. By the Carboniferous period, from 360 million to 286 million years ago, many of these land-dwelling arthropods had grown spectacularly—and one spider had a body 20 inches long.

▶ *Acarina.* A close relative of the modern moss mite, this arachnid may have fed on rotting vegetation.

Eurypterid

Fossils of eurypterids *(left)*, sometimes called sea scorpions, have been found from North America to Europe to Australia. These Silurian arthropods lived in bays and brackish water, but tracks found in Australia indicate that they may also have been among the first creatures to venture onto dry land. Equipped with several pairs of spiny walking legs and large paddles for swimming, eurypterids ranged in size from a few inches to several feet long.

▲ **Paleocaronoid.** This ticklike arachnid lived off the body fluids of other creatures.

◄ **Rhyniella.** Possibly the oldest fossil insect, the chubby, segmented front portion of *Rhyniella* was discovered in ancient Scottish rocks from the Devonian period, 360 to 408 million years ago.

Scorpion

Related to eurypterids, scorpions *(shown in a Silurian fossil, right)* are among the first true land creatures found in the fossil record. By the Silurian period these arachnids, which may have lived in the water early in their evolution, had developed powerful pincers, stout walking legs, and long tail-like telsons capable of injecting poison. They breathed with book lungs, indicating that they took their oxygen from the air rather than the water.

When Did Plants Appear on Land?

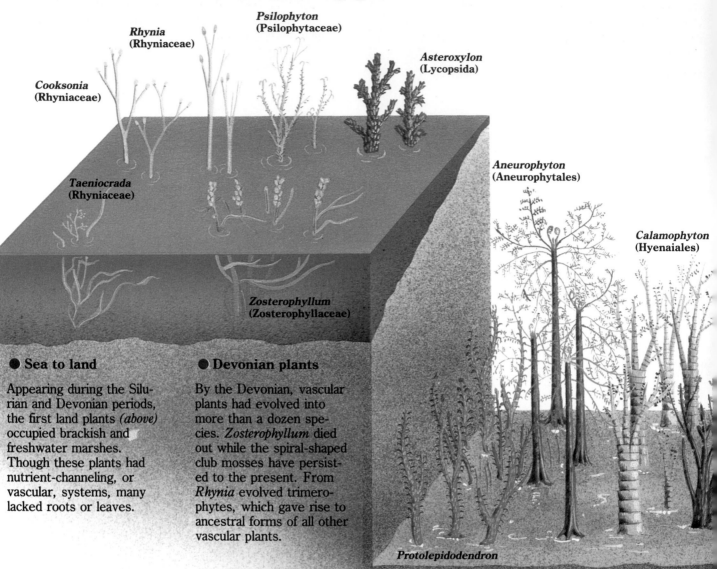

Cooksonia (Rhyniaceae)

Rhynia (Rhyniaceae)

Psilophyton (Psilophytaceae)

Asteroxylon (Lycopsida)

Taeniocrada (Rhyniaceae)

Aneurophyton (Aneurophytales)

Calamophyton (Hyenaiales)

Zosterophyllum (Zosterophyllaceae)

Protolepidodendron

● **Sea to land**

Appearing during the Silurian and Devonian periods, the first land plants *(above)* occupied brackish and freshwater marshes. Though these plants had nutrient-channeling, or vascular, systems, many lacked roots or leaves.

● **Devonian plants**

By the Devonian, vascular plants had evolved into more than a dozen species. *Zosterophyllum* died out while the spiral-shaped club mosses have persisted to the present. From *Rhynia* evolved trimerophytes, which gave rise to ancestral forms of all other vascular plants.

The coal-forming forests of the Carboniferous (Mississippian/Pennsylvanian) period left behind many fossils of early plants. Evidence of such plants as *Annularia (near right),* a rush that favored swampy areas, and *Lepidodendron (far right),* a large treelike plant, indicates that the Carboniferous period was quite warm and wet.

Annularia (imprint of stem)

Lepidodendron

The ancestors of today's land plants were probably green algae. Exposed to dry periods by retreating inland seas, these tiny plants developed a waxy layer to prevent water loss, and stomata, or pores, to take carbon dioxide from the air. Where the plant stems touched mud, cells grew out and anchored the plants, absorbing nourishment. Tissues called xylem then evolved to move nutrients through the plant, followed, eventually, by roots. By such a process, scientists believe the first vascular plants arose.

Silurian rocks hold fossils of vascular plants, or Tracheophyta, reedy plants without true roots or leaves. In the early Devonian, Lycopsida, plants with roots, stems, and leaves, appeared. All were spore producers. Progymnosperms had already emerged—forebears of early seed plants, including conifers, which still flourish today.

Plants developed during the Devonian period whose spores gave rise to gametophytes, tiny plants with both male and female organs. Sperm from the male organs fertilized the female organs.

Male organ
Microspore
Female organ
Macrospore

By the Carboniferous period, seed ferns like *Neuropteris (right)* had a more advanced form of reproduction *(left)*. The young plant that resulted was protected in a seed.

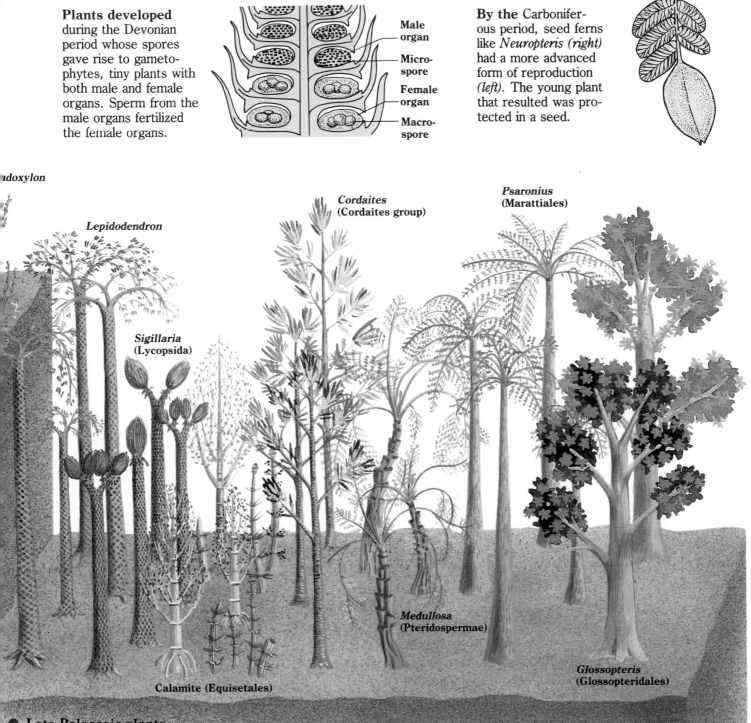

adoxylon

Lepidodendron

Sigillaria
(Lycopsida)

Cordaites
(Cordaites group)

Psaronius
(Marattiales)

Calamite (Equisetales)

Medullosa
(Pteridospermae)

Glossopteris
(Glossopteridales)

● Late Paleozoic plants

In the moist, warm Carboniferous period, the ancestors of ferns, horsetails, club mosses, and seed bearers grew into larger forms. Dense forests of giant spore producers such as *Lepidodendron* and early seed bearers such as *Medullosa* stretched across the lowlands of the continents. When the cooler Permian period began, the swamps started to dry up and *Lepidodendron* and other Carboniferous plants disappeared. In their place appeared such cold-adapted genuses as *Glossopteris* and the early conifers.

Which Creatures Were First to Fly?

The first fliers were arthropods. Once insects evolved wings, they succeeded in escaping spiders, scorpions, and other predators. Wings began, one theory goes, as tissue flaps, used for gliding, on the thoraxes of leaping insects. Later, as muscles around these flaps strengthened, the flaps enlarged and became papery and veined with spiny supports. Eventually—by the Carboniferous period, according to the fossil record—they had developed into full-fledged wings.

There was one drawback to the new flying structures, however. They prevented the paleopterans, or "ancient wings," as these prehistoric insects are called, from hiding. Thus emerged the neopterans, or "new wings"—insects whose resting wings nested neatly on their backsides, tucked out of sight.

Meganeura. The ancestor of modern-day dragonflies, *Meganeura* swept the skies 300 million years ago with four wings, each about a foot long. Attached to its 15-inch body were three pairs of claw-bearing legs that the insect used to draw prey into its well-developed jaw.

Stenodictya. This primitive flier retained two stubby tissue flaps *(green),* from which insect wings are thought to have developed.

Miscoptera. Once believed to be amphibious—adapted to both land and water—*Miscoptera* is now considered a flying land insect.

Protophasma. Folding wings put this predecessor of the cockroach and praying mantis among the more highly evolved neopterans.

How Did Amphibians Evolve?

The warm, humid Devonian period, 408 million to 360 million years ago, changed many lakes into plant-choked, oxygen-poor swamps. One order of bony fish called Rhipidistia evolved traits that were well suited to these marshy habitats, including lungs and muscular fins supported by bones.

By swimming to the surface, Rhipidistia genuses like *Eusthenopteron* were able to rise above the water to gulp air. Gradually, perhaps tempted by prey on dry land or driven by drought, *Eusthenopteron* learned to waddle its way onto land or to nearby water holes. The first known amphibian, the predator called *Ichthyostega*—a vertebrate that was at home both in water and on land—is believed to have descended from these lobe-finned fish.

● **Eusthenopteron**

Eusthenopteron's bony fins doubled as stubby legs when its watery habitat dried up. Wriggling and crawling, the 2-foot-long amphibian ancestor would seek out a new pond, drawing air into its lung through tiny nostrils. Once in the water, the fish swam after prey with its powerful tail.

From fish to amphibian

Fish evolution began over 80 million years before the arrival of rhipidistians—the order of fish that fathered amphibians. In the Cambrian period came the jawless agnathans, followed in the Silurian by the primitive jawed gnathostomes—the now-vanished Acanthodii. In the early Devonian, the placoderms, Osteichthyes, or bony fish, and Chrondrichthyes, or cartilaginous fish, appeared.

The Osteichthyes included two major groups of fish: the actinopterygians, or ray-fins—the forerunners of modern fish; and the mostly extinct sarcopterygians, or lobe-finned fish—the great-grandparents of amphibians. The lobe-fins were of two types, the Dipteriformes, or lungfish, and the crossopterygians, which included the coelacanths and the rhipidistians. It was the rhipidistians who played ancestor to *Ichthyostega*, the first known amphibian.

		Paleozoic era	
Ordovician period	**Silurian period**	**Devonian period**	**Carbonifer**
Superclass Agnatha		*Cephalaspis*	
	Class Placodermi	*Coccosteus*	
		Class Chondrichthyes	
			Cladoselach
	Class Acanthodii	*Climatius*	
		Subclass Actinopterygii	
	Class Osteichthyes		*Cheirolepis*
			Dipterus
	Subclass Sarcopterygii		
		Eusthenopteron	
	Class Amphibia		
		Ichthyostega	

Well-developed gill plate cover (operculum)

Still more fish than amphibian, *Eusthenopteron* retained the gill plates (opercula) typical of lobe-fins and hid its limb bones inside fleshy fins.

Reduced operculum

Gill plates had all but disappeared in *Ichthyostega*, whose bones permitted greater movement than did *Eusthenopteron*'s.

● *Ichthyostega*

Though it differed markedly in appearance from its ancestor, 5-foot-long *Ichthyostega* retained many rhipidistian skeletal features. Lobe-fin bones became larger and limbs more flexible as the animal adapted to land. The amphibian's nerve cord was encased in a strengthened backbone, which was fused to the pelvic girdle for improved hind-leg strength. Subtler changes included a distinct neck.

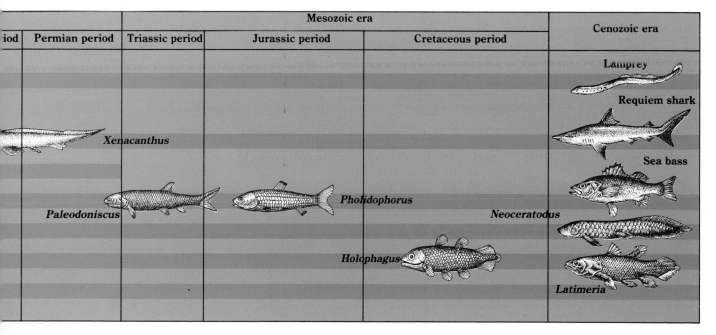

iod	Permian period	Triassic period	Jurassic period	Cretaceous period	Cenozoic era
			Mesozoic era		
					Lamprey
					Requiem shark
	Xenacanthus				Sea bass
			Pholidophorus		*Neoceratodus*
	Paleodoniscus				
			Holophagus		*Latimeria*

Are Reptiles Related to Amphibians?

After the first amphibians lumbered out of the water in the late Devonian period, they quickly spread throughout the Earth's equatorial regions. The small lepospondyls lived in ponds, while the larger, hunting labyrinthodonts like *Ichthyostega* claimed the wet flatlands.

Challengers in the form of reptiles appeared within a few million years, however. The details of their amphibian ancestry remain vague, but reptiles seem to have evolved as they adapted to an environment left vacant by shore-bound amphibians. Unlike amphibians, who had to return to the water to lay their larva-forming eggs, reptiles laid their hard-shelled eggs on land—and left them to hatch into air-breathing reptiles.

▼ *Hylonomus* is the oldest known reptile. It was 3 feet in length.

▶ *Proterogyrinus* was a 5-foot-long anthracosaur—a possible ancestor of reptiles.

▼ *Eogyrinus,* an amphibian, walked on four weak limbs.

▲ *Seymouria's* skeleton was more reptilian than amphibian, but it had amphibian ear notches.

▼ *Diplocaulus,* an amphibian, seldom left the water.

◀ *Mesosaurus* lived in the fresh water, where it swam with the aid of its long tail, using its feet for steering.

Amphibians

Amphibians were heavy and slow.

They laid jellylike eggs in water, where the eggs hatched into gill-breathing larvae.

The amphibian heart had three chambers. It was slightly more evolved than those of fish.

Reptiles

Reptiles ran easily on agile legs.

They laid hard-shelled eggs, from which emerged lung-breathing young.

Crocodiles, which are reptiles, had efficient four-chambered hearts.

◀ *Edaphosaurus,* a plant-eating reptile, was a likely prey of *Dimetrodon (below, right).*

▼ *Dimetrodon,* a mammal-like reptile, had three rows of razor-sharp reptilian teeth, which it used to kill and eat its prey.

▲ *Eryops,* king of amphibians, had an armored breastplate and heavily muscled legs that made it a formidable predator in the early Permian.

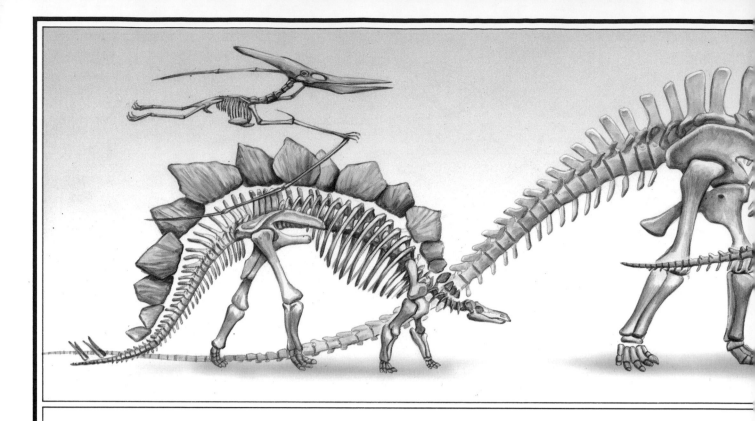

4
When Dinosaurs Ruled

The age of reptiles began and ended with two of the greatest mass extinctions in the history of planet Earth. When the Mesozoic era dawned, about 245 million years ago, the Earth's continents had recently drifted together into a single huge landmass called Pangaea. As a result, the climate began to change and up to 78% of all living genuses vanished.

About 180 million years later, the Mesozoic era, or time of the middle animals, came to a close as Pangaea was well into its slow crumble into separate continents. By this time, some 65

million years ago, every large land animal—including all of the various dinosaurs—and all marine reptiles had become extinct.

For 140 million years, dinosaurs—ranging from chicken-size predators to huge flesh-eaters and gigantic plant-eaters—dominated the Earth. Other reptiles, birds, and mammals were present, but in small numbers. Dinosaurs' fossilized skeletons tell us when and how they lived and when they died. But fossils do not tell us why dinosaurs suddenly became extinct at the end of the Mesozoic era. Some scientists believe that the extinction was due primarily to gradual changes in the planet's climate. Other researchers suspect a more dramatic cause: the impact of a gigantic meteorite or comet that crashed into the Earth. The resulting dust and smoke would have blotted out the sun's light, causing an extended, fatal winter.

Dinosaurs were immensely successful animals, stalking the Earth for more than 140 million years.

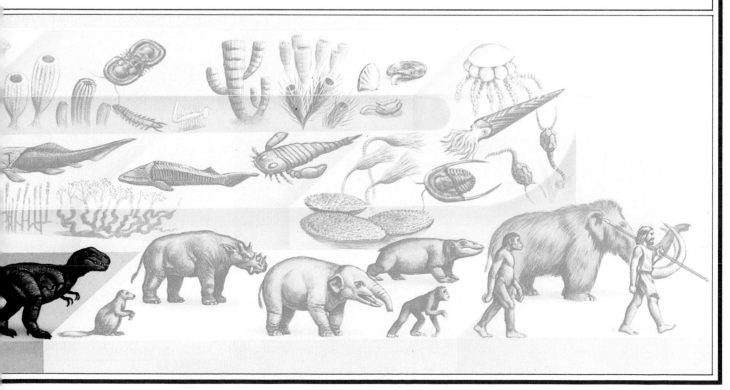

What Were Early Reptiles Like?

About 260 million years ago, Earth's continents drifted into a single landmass called Pangaea, causing the extinction of many species. Reptiles, however, survived and began an evolutionary eruption, spreading throughout the land, air, and sea. The most numerous, called mammal-like reptiles, started an evolutionary line leading to mammals. Others were ancestors of modern reptiles. And from some reptile lines evolved the various kinds of dinosaurs. This age when reptiles began to thrive is called the Triassic period, the first of three parts of the Mesozoic era.

▼ **Hylonomus.** One of the earliest known reptiles, this animal probably ate insects.

▼ **Cynognathus.** Th mammal-like reptile probably had hair a whiskers.

► **Tanystropheus.** Almost all neck, this animal lived in water.

▼ **Henodus.** This reptile had a horny beak instead of teeth.

► **Euparkeria.** A small dinosaur relative.

▲ **Proganochelys.** This was an ancestor of turtles.

▼ **Mixosaurus.** This ichthyosaur, or "fish reptile," was a fast swimmer and probably hunted fish.

Nothosaurus. Unrelated to dinosaurs, these 12-foot-long marine reptiles used their sharp teeth to catch fish.

Placodus. These marine reptiles had large platelike teeth.

The reptile family tree

Beginning as lizardlike animals similar to *Hylonomus*, the reptile class grew to dominate Earth by the late Permian period and spawned the largest land animals that ever lived, the dinosaurs. The family tree evolved four main branches. Fossil specialists decide which branch an animal belonged to by looking for special openings in the skull.

The first branch to form, called Anapsida, included *Hylonomus* and gave rise to turtles and tortoises. The second branch, Synapsida, included the mammal-like reptiles, ancestors of modern mammals. Third came the Diapsida, which split again, giving rise to lizards and snakes on one hand, and dinosaurs, crocodiles, and birds on the other. Last was the Euryapsida, which included many marine reptiles. All euryapsids had become extinct by the end of the Mesozoic era.

▼ **Scaphonyx.** This pig-size reptile ate plants.

▶ **Eudimorphodon.** This primitive winged reptile soared on 3-foot wings.

▶ **Plateosaurus.** The 26-foot-long *Plateosaurus* stood on two legs to feed.

◀ **Lystrosaurus.** This mammal-like reptile ate plants.

▼ **Protosuchus.** This early crocodile had long legs and a short snout.

▲ **Icarosaurus.** An early ancestor of modern lizards and snakes, *Icarosaurus* would glide through the air on its winglike membrane.

	Carboniferous period	Permian period	Triassic period	Jurassic period	Cretaceous period	Cenozoic era
Subclass Anapsida			Order Mesosauria	Order Captorhinida		Order Chelonida
Subclass Synapsida		Order Pelycosauria	Order Therapsida			
Subclass Euryapsida				Order Ichthyosauria / Order Plesiosauria / Order Placodontia / Family Araeoscelidae		
Subclass Diapsida			Order Thecodontia	Order Squamata / Order Sphenodonta / Order Eosuchia / Order Crocodylia / Order Saurischia / Order Ornithischia / Order Pterosauria		

Carboniferous period	Permian period	Triassic period	Jurassic period	Cretaceous period	Cenozoic era
Paleozoic era			Mesozoic era		Cenozoic era

What Were Mammal-like Reptiles?

Shortly after the first reptile appeared on land, a new evolutionary branch arose: the mammal-like reptiles. Over about 100 million years, these animals may have evolved hair and an internally controlled body temperature. Some ate plants. Others spent cool nights eating insects while cold-blooded reptiles remained sluggish. In the late Triassic period, over 200 million years ago, a final split took place, and true mammals arose. These shrew-size animals held their own until the dinosaurs became extinct, then began to spread across the land, into the sea, and into the air.

Cynognathus. Strong, doglike jaws helped this 200-pound flesh-eater tear into its prey. Hair probably covered its body, helping to control its internal temperature.

Living in burrows

Some fossil skeletons have been found curled up in underground burrows. Scientists believe these animals slept in chambers dug out of the ground.

Diademodon. Paleontologists have found fossils of a mammal-like reptile, a cynodont called *Diademodon,* curled up as if sleeping.

Mammal-like reptiles

Starting from a group of small reptiles called pelycosaurs, the family tree of the mammal-like reptiles, or synapsids, split into one other branch, the therapsids. Each branch split again into smaller branches. From predatory pelycosaurs arose the sail-backed edaphosaurs, the first known plant-eating vertebrates. Using plants as food, edaphosaurs formed the front lines of the land-dwelling vertebrates. With edaphosaurs as a food source, a new branch of predatory pelycosaurs evolved. *Dimetrodon* and its relatives evolved their own skin-covered sails. By catching sunlight with the sail, *Dimetrodon* and *Edaphosaurus* could warm up. By turning the sail away from the sun, they could cool off. The second major branch, called therapsids, produced more branches; from one of these sprouted modern mammals.

Carboniferous

Suborder
Ophiacodontia

Suborder
Sphenaco-
dontoidea

Suborder
Edaphosauria

Order
Pelycosauria

Oligokyphus. With their specialized chewing teeth, tritylodont (three-knobbed teeth) reptiles survived after mammals evolved.

Probainognathus. Fossils of *Probainognathus* show a jaw midway between that of the weak-jawed, reptilelike therapsids and powerful-jawed advanced mammals.

The first true mammals

The first mammals appeared on Earth about 215 million years ago during the late Triassic period of the Mesozoic era. These small, ratlike creatures grew fur, chewed with modern jaws, and might have nursed their young.

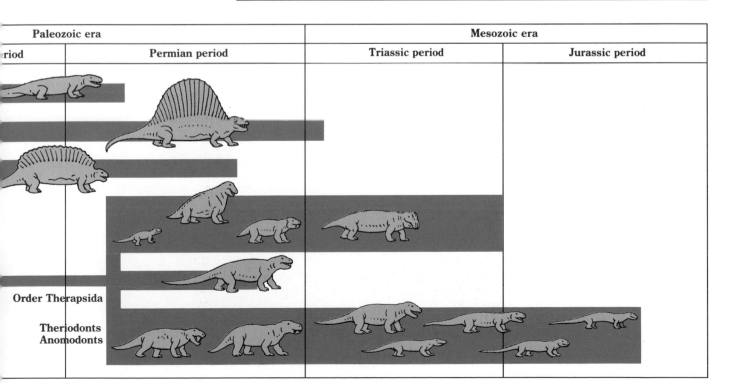

	Paleozoic era		Mesozoic era	
...riod	Permian period		Triassic period	Jurassic period
Order Therapsida				
Theriodonts Anomodonts				

Where Did Dinosaurs Come From?

About 260 million years ago, an evolutionary line of low-slung, mostly dog-size reptiles called thecodonts broke away from other diapsid groups. With their quick legs and strong, socketed teeth, the thecodont line thrived, giving rise to modern crocodiles, the winged reptiles called pterosaurs, and the most famous Mesozoic animals of all, the dinosaurs.

By the middle Triassic, 30 million years later, thecodonts shared the landscape with a vast array of dinosaurs, from little predators trotting on two legs to 4-ton giants jolting the ground with each step. Within a few million years—shortly into the Jurassic—thecodonts, as well as most mammal-like reptiles, had succumbed to climatic changes and the wave of dinosaurs, the "terrible lizards."

Coelophysis. Light and graceful but a fierce predator, *Coelophysis (near right)* sped along on its slender hind legs. Ten feet long, it was a primitive member of the lizard-hipped dinosaurs, one of the two major groups of dinosaurs.

Euparkeria. This 3-foot-long ancestor of dinosaurs *(above left)* lived during the Triassic period. An advanced thecodont in the group called pseudosuchians (false crocodiles), *Euparkeria* may have occasionally run on its hind legs.

The dinosaur family tree

From the thecodont line came four evolutionary groups or orders. The crocodile line split off about 235 million years ago, in the middle Triassic period, carrying on a body plan that survives to this day. Primitive thecodonts survived until the end of the Triassic. Meanwhile, the winged pterosaurs split off about 220 million years ago, in the late Triassic. Two distinct lines of dinosaurs had appeared by the dawn of the Jurassic, about 12 million years later. Bird-hipped dinosaurs eventually included the familiar *Stegosaurus* and *Triceratops.* The lizard-hipped dinosaurs included both the giant plant-eaters such as *Apatosaurus*—at 30 tons, one of the largest land animals ever—and both small and large predators, such as the fearsome *Tyrannosaurus.* Modern birds may have evolved from a branch of the lizard-hipped dinosaurs that split off during the middle Jurassic.

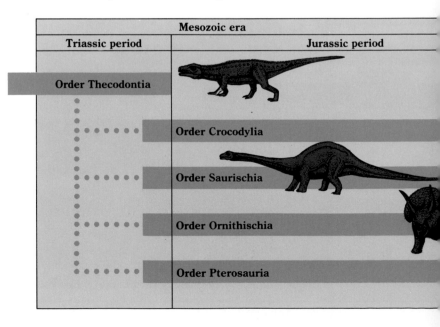

Mesozoic era	
Triassic period	**Jurassic period**
Order Thecodontia	
	Order Crocodylia
	Order Saurischia
	Order Ornithischia
	Order Pterosauria

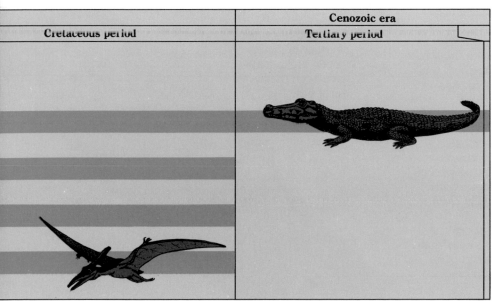

Ornithosuchus. One of the most advanced pseudosuchians, this thecodont lived in the middle and late Triassic period. Some scientists think this sharp-toothed predator was one of the first true dinosaurs.

Cretaceous period	Cenozoic era
	Tertiary period

Legs of various reptiles

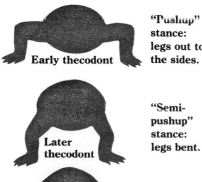

Early thecodont

"Pushup" stance: legs out to the sides.

Later thecodont

"Semi-pushup" stance: legs bent.

Dinosaur

"Pillar" stance: legs under body.

What Were the First Birds?

The first clues to a missing link between dinosaurs and birds appeared in 1861. The imprint of a feather and then a complete fossil showing the skeleton of an 18-inch-long dinosaur with the feathers of a bird turned up in rocks 150 million years old. Named *Archaeopteryx,* or "ancient wing," this weak flier held sway as the oldest bird until 1983, when bones of what may be an older bird were found in Texas. These poorly preserved fossils—named *Protoavis,* or "first bird"—were found in rocks 75 million years older than those holding *Archaeopteryx.*

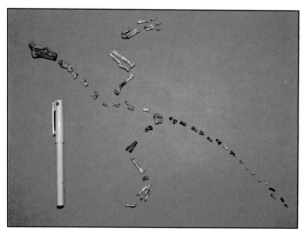

The fossilized remains of two adult *Protoavis* have been discovered.

The crow-size *Protoavis* lived during the middle Triassic.

How did flight evolve in birds?

Paleontologists propose two pathways for the evolution of flight in birds. Both begin with small lizard-hipped dinosaurs. Tiny, tree-climbing dinosaurs may have evolved feathers on their forelegs. These feathers would have helped the lizardlike insect-eaters leap and glide from branch to branch. The longer a dinosaur's feathers, the better it was able to glide and the more likely it was to pass on its genes to the next generation.

A second theory has birds evolving from small dinosaurs that ran on two legs, leaping and snatching at insects that were flying near the ground. Feathers may have helped hold in body heat at first. Later bird ancestors may have netted insects from the air with their feathered forelegs. A dinosaur that was able to leap and glide briefly could catch even more insects.

No matter which evolutionary path proves correct, full-fledged flight would have freed birds from the ground entirely, opening up new territory in which to feed, nest, and hide from predators.

From dinosaur to *Protoavis*

A small tree-climbing dinosaur in the lizard-hipped group may have been the ancestor of birds.

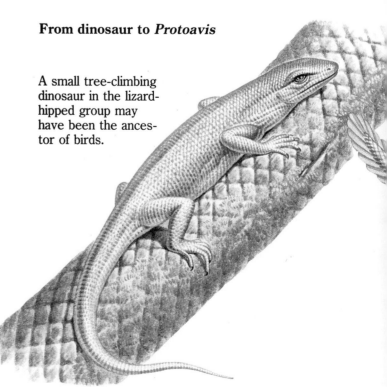

Both *Archaeopteryx* and *Protoavis* bones show many dinosaur-like features. Clawed fingers, a bony tail, and at least some teeth appear in both fossils. But both also show some birdlike features, including a skull with large eye sockets and a large braincase like those of modern birds.

This imagined gliding dinosaur is halfway between tree-climbers and birds.

Perhaps the oldest bird fossil, *Protoavis* may have begun the evolutionary line leading to birds 225 million years ago.

What Was *Archaeopteryx* Like?

In August 1861 German quarry workers discovered a remarkable fossil—the impression of a single feather in pale, smooth rock 150 million years old. The feather fossil caused a lot of excitement among scientists because it was the earliest bird fossil known. But a month later, scientists found something even more thrilling: a feathered skeleton, missing only the skull, and in 1877 they found a complete skeleton.

Five skeletons have been found altogether, several surrounded by impressions of feathers. But the shapes of the skeletons are those of dinosaurs, not birds. This fossil mixture of dinosaur and bird features was named *Archaeopteryx*. It remained the earliest bird known until *Protoavis* was discovered in 1983.

Archaeopteryx was about 18 inches long.

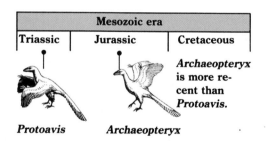

Mesozoic era		
Triassic	Jurassic	Cretaceous

Archaeopteryx is more recent than *Protoavis*.

Protoavis   Archaeopteryx

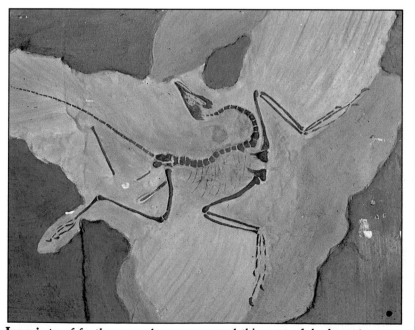

Imprints of feathers can be seen around this cast of *Archaeopteryx*.

Dinosaurs, *Archaeopteryx,* and birds

Archaeopteryx shared many features with certain small dinosaurs. Both had short bodies, flexible necks, three-fingered hands, toothed jaws, and long, bony tails. Both also had the long legs of swift runners and solid bones, not the hollow ones of modern birds. But *Archaeopteryx* also had some birdlike features. Its feet, though not as advanced as those of a modern perching bird, would have been able to grasp branches. It also had a fused collarbone, the "wishbone" of modern birds that braces the shoulders while the bird flaps its wings, making flight possible. *Archaeopteryx* could probably fly, perhaps swooping down on fish from cliffs along the shore. It was an evolutionary dead end, however, eventually losing out to its lighter cousins, the true birds.

Was *Archaeopteryx* an active flier, merely a glider, or did it run along the ground netting insects with its outstretched wings? No one knows for sure. Its wing feathers have an asymmetrical shape like those of modern flying birds. But it lacked the deep breastbone, or keel, of birds. Powerful flight muscles require a keel as an anchor, so it seems likely that *Archaeopteryx* was a weak flier at best.

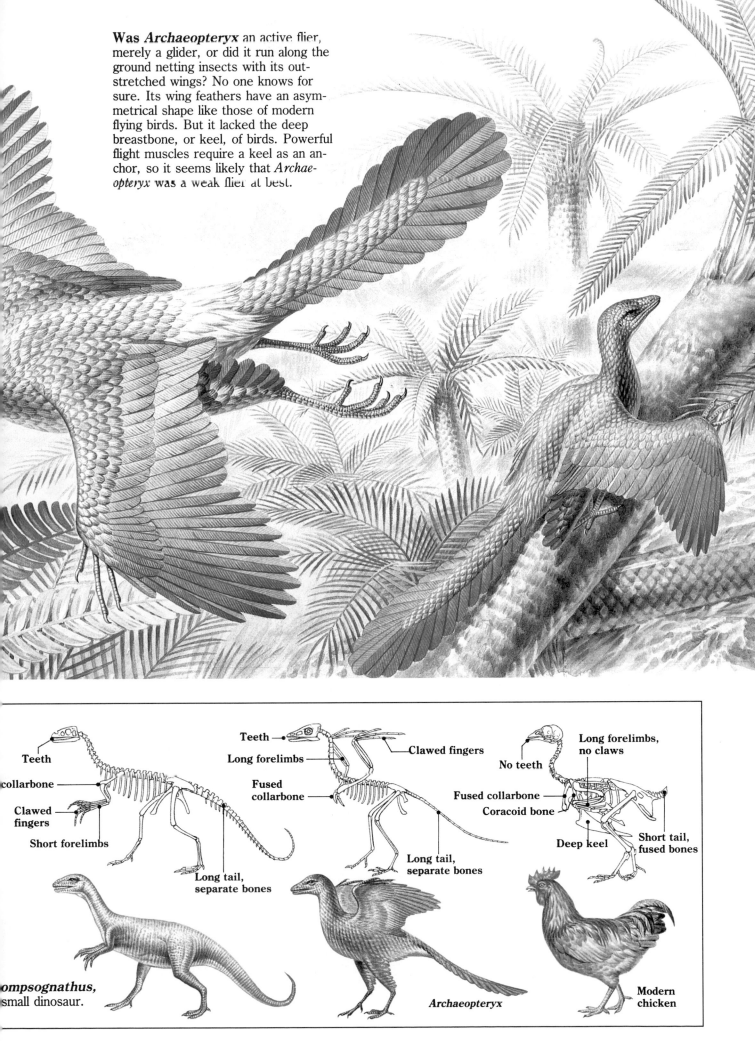

Teeth

collarbone

Clawed fingers

Short forelimbs

ompsognathus, small dinosaur.

Teeth

Long forelimbs

Fused collarbone

Clawed fingers

Long tail, separate bones

Archaeopteryx

No teeth

Fused collarbone

Coracoid bone

Deep keel

Long forelimbs, no claws

Short tail, fused bones

Modern chicken

How Did Mammals Evolve?

The dawn of the dinosaurs in the late Triassic period, 215 million years ago, brought dramatic changes to the Earth. Mammal-like reptiles had dominated the landscape for 70 million years but now became food for hungry flesh-eating dinosaurs. Within about 10 million years, all that was left of the mammal-like reptile line were the mammals themselves.

Not much larger than mice, these fur-covered, warm-blooded animals foraged for food—insects and worms and perhaps seeds—at night. During the day they used their small size to avoid predatory flesh-eating reptiles by hiding in crevices or burrows. For 140 million years, mammals lived in the shadow of the dinosaurs. While their body shape changed little, these tiny mammals evolved better brains, sharper senses, and cleverer behavior. When dinosaurs disappeared 65 million years ago, mammals were ready to take over the Earth.

The first mammals

Mammals evolved from the mammal-like therapsids during the late Triassic period, about 215 million years ago. Because their teeth featured three small cone shapes, scientists named these shrew-size mammals triconodonts. One such mammal was *Morganucodon (left),* a 4-inch nocturnal animal that may have relied on smell to find its insect prey.

Near the end of the Triassic period the triconodont branch may have grown two sprouts. The first survived the Jurassic and split into two lines during the early Cretaceous period, about 130 million years ago. The metatherian twig evolved into modern marsupials, pouched mammals such as the kangaroo. The eutherian twig evolved into mammals with a placenta but no pouch.

Mammal ancestor

Cynognathus crateronotus, its fossil skull shown at left, was a large cynodont, an ancestor of mammals. Living in the early Triassic period, this flesh-eater had teeth resembling those of mammals—stabbing, or "canine," teeth in front as well as incisors and molars.

How Were Dinosaurs Related?

The animals we call dinosaurs actually consisted of two quite different groups. Both sprang out of the thecodont evolutionary line—the same line that gave rise to crocodiles and pterosaurs. The lizard-hipped dinosaurs, or saurischians, had pelvic bones that were arranged in the same way as those of modern reptiles. Order Saurischia included the flesh-eaters, large and small, and also the giant plant-eaters. Bird-hipped dinosaurs, or ornithischians, had pelvic bones arranged like those of modern birds. Order Ornithischia included four groups of large plant-eaters.

Hypsilophodon: Cretaceous period.

Heterodontosaurus: early-Jurassic-period plant-eater.

Kentrosaurus: late Jurassic.

■ Order Ornithischia

Ilium

Ischium

Pubis

Stegosaurus skeleton

In the ornithischians, the hipbone, or pubis, points backward, parallel to the ischium. Nearly all of these dinosaurs ate plants, many using a horny, toothless beak.

Lesothosaurus: late Triassic to early Jurassic periods.

■ Order Saurischia

Tyrannosaurus skeleton

Ilium

Ischium

Pubis

In the saurischians, the pubis points downward and forward, away from the ischium. This order includes the two-legged theropods—flesh-eaters of all sizes—and the huge, plant-eating sauropods.

Ornitholestes: a small, late-Jurassic flesh-eater.

Allosaurus: large Jurassic flesh-eater.

Compsognathus: a small, late-Jurassic flesh-eater.

Struthiomimus: Cretaceous period.

74

Hylaeosaurus: Cretaceous.

Anchiceratops: late Cretaceous period.

Stegoceras: Cretaceous period.

Iguanodon: early Cretaceous period.

Ouranosaurus: Cretaceous period.

Tenontosaurus: Cretaceous period.

Camarasaurus: late-Jurassic plant-eater.

Ultrasaurus: late-Jurassic plant-eater, perhaps the largest dinosaur.

Ceratosaurus: Jurassic flesh-eater.

What Did Dinosaurs Eat?

Sometimes dinosaur fossils turn up with preserved food inside. This shows scientists at least one of the foods the dinosaur ate while alive. For instance, scientists found one *Compsognathus* skeleton with the skeleton of a small reptile inside it; some hadrosaur fossils have held twigs and cones.

But even a skeleton can tell a paleontologist something about the dinosaur's diet. Long, sharp, slashing teeth belong to flesh-eaters. Rows of flat teeth would have served plant-eaters well in chopping their tough food. Long, heavy lower jawbones work best for nipping at plants. And the shape of a dinosaur's neck can indicate whether it ate upright or foraged along the ground.

Parasaurolophus

Parasaurolophus and other hadrosaurs used their hard, horny beaks to snap off tough twigs in low tree branches and browse along the ground. Behind their beaks grew hundreds of flat grinding teeth.

Parasaurolophus skull. Rows of flat teeth were continuously replaced from below.

Brachiosaurus

Like a gigantic giraffe, *Brachiosaurus* probably nipped the tops of tall tree-size plants. To support one of the largest dinosaur bodies, it probably ate tons of coarse food every day and slowly digested the food in a huge intestine—the way that elephants do today.

Brachiosaurus skull. With its large, chisel-shaped teeth, *Brachiosaurus* probably ate tough plants but didn't chew its food.

Tyrannosaurus

The 7-ton *Tyrannosaurus* ranks as one of the most feared villains of the prehistoric world—in movies and cartoons, at least. But some scientists suspect the so-called tyrant reptile ate only dead or dying animals, the way modern vultures do. One huge carcass every few weeks may have kept *Tyrannosaurus* full. Those seemingly useless front feet may have helped it rise up after resting on the ground.

Tyrannosaurus skull. Sixty replaceable teeth up to 7 inches long line the jaws of this skull. Each tooth has serrated edges like a steak knife—ideal for tearing off huge bites of flesh.

Baryonyx skull. With 128 sharp, serrated teeth in its long snout, *Baryonyx* could have snatched slippery fish.

Oviraptor skull. *Oviraptor* had a hard, toothless beak, a lightweight skull, and a large braincase.

● Oviraptor

Because one fossil skeleton was directly over a nest of *Protoceratops* eggs, scientists dubbed this small, birdlike dinosaur *Oviraptor,* or "egg thief."

Baryonyx

Baryonyx may have snared fish with its 12-inch-long front claw and held them in its crocodile-like snout.

How Did Dinosaurs Reproduce?

In 1923 a team led by paleontologist Roy Chapman Andrews dug up the first fossil dinosaur eggs ever discovered. The 8-inch-long *Protoceratops* eggs lay in bowl-shaped, fossilized nests once scooped from sandy soil. These and many other dinosaur nests led scientists to believe that most dinosaurs laid eggs much as modern sea turtles do. In some dinosaur nests, many eggs lie arranged in layers, as if several females used the same nest. And at a site in Montana, a group of dinosaurs—called *Maiasaura*—seem to have nested together in a colony, like modern seabirds.

Protoceratops. This plant-eater probably lived in herds. Fossils of adults, young, and eggs occur together.

How big were dinosaur eggs?

Because some dinosaurs were truly giants, you might expect their eggs to be gigantic too. But of all the fossilized dinosaur eggs found, the largest is only about a foot long—just twice the size of an ostrich egg and smaller than the largest fossilized bird egg discovered (see comparisons in diagram at right). As an egg gets larger, its shell must get thicker or it would break under its own weight. The shell of a gigantic egg would be so thick the baby dinosaur couldn't get out. The 12-inch eggs of *Hypselosaurus* had shells nearly ⅛-inch thick. *Maiasaura* laid eggs about 8 inches long. Most medium-size dinosaurs probably laid eggs the size of modern turkey eggs.

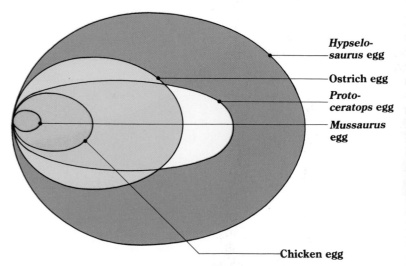

Hypselo-saurus egg

Ostrich egg

Proto-ceratops egg

Mussaurus egg

Chicken egg

Oviraptor. This dinosaur
was discovered near a *Protoceratops* nest. It probably ate
mollusks and eggs.

What's inside a dinosaur egg?

Early dinosaur eggshells were leathery and water-
proof, like those of most modern reptiles, but later
eggs may have been more like crocodile or bird
eggs. Like the shell of chicken eggs, the later dinosaur eggshell contained calcium carbonate, the
same chemical found in seashells. Some dinosaurs
may have kept their eggs within their bodies until
they hatched, the way some modern snakes do.
The young would have been born alive. In some
fossil nests, skeletons of newly hatched young lie
alongside unhatched eggs. And, using special x-ray
techniques borrowed from medicine, the discover-
ers of the *Maiasaura* nesting colony photographed
the skeleton of a dinosaur still in its egg.

Fossilized egg

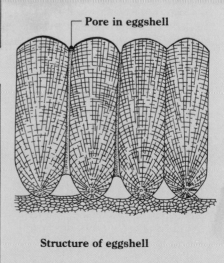

Pore in eggshell

Structure of eggshell

Cold- or Warm-Blooded?

The popular image of dinosaurs shows them as slow, stupid, and cold-blooded, like modern reptiles. But recently some scientists have challenged that stereotype, using several strong arguments. The spectacular discovery of a dinosaur nesting area, with eggs, young, and adults all situated in one area, hints that dinosaurs may have formed social groups and cared for their young as modern warm-blooded animals, the birds and mammals, do.

By looking closely at fossil skeletons, paleontologists have found other similarities between dinosaurs and warm-blooded animals. Dinosaurs walked with their legs directly under the body, not splay-legged like modern reptiles. And the number of flesh-eaters compared with the number of their prey matches the pattern seen in modern warm-blooded predators.

Reptile temperature control

Modern reptiles burn a fraction of the food to keep warm that mammals and birds do. They control their temperature in another way. To warm up, a cold lizard will slowly spread out in the sun, darken its skin slightly, and bask. Once warm, reptiles become active, scuttling or slithering after food. If they become too hot, they slither into shade or water—they can't sweat. In cooler climates, reptiles become sluggish at night and hibernate in winter. Being cold-blooded has costs, but it saves fuel. Reptiles need about a tenth as much food as birds or mammals do.

Marine iguanas, large lizards of the Galápagos Islands, off Ecuador, eat seaweed. To warm up, they cling to sun-baked rocks.

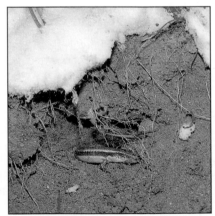

In cool parts of the world, lizards cannot maintain a body temperature that allows activity in winter, so they hibernate.

Troödon. A large brain, eyes that faced forward, and apparent social behavior have given *Troödon* a reputation as the smartest dinosaur. Hunting in packs made the flesh-eating *Troödon* a dangerous predator.

Armored and cool

Stegosaurus, a 20-foot-long plant-eater, had a brain the size of a small potato. Large back plates may have helped control its temperature.

In 1877 a paleontologist dug out the first fossil skeleton of *Stegosaurus.* But along with the skeleton came a puzzle: several diamond-shaped plates up to 3 feet long. At first the scientist thought these plates were like the scales of a turtle, but he later arranged them upright along the spine. No one knew their purpose. And how did they grow? Vertically in a row, vertically in two rows, alternating, or flopped over sideways?

Scientists now think the plates formed a heat exchanger. Wind blowing past the plates—arranged in two vertical rows alternating down the back—would cool the blood in the flesh that covered the plates. Sunlight striking the plates would heat them up. Blood vessels carried heat to or from the plates. The bony plates probably also served as armor, protecting the slow *Stegosaurus* from attack.

Warm-blooded thermostats

Birds and mammals maintain body temperature by burning extra food. Up to 80% of that food goes to keeping warm. But this process is like a heater that's always on. To cool off, warm-blooded animals combine behavior and heat exchange just as reptiles do. Humans sweat, cooling blood vessels under the skin. Elephants wave their ears. Dogs and birds pant, releasing heat from moist mouths and lungs. Air sacs connected to birds' lungs add even more surface area for exchanging heat. Even cold-blooded crocodiles hold their mouths open to release heat.

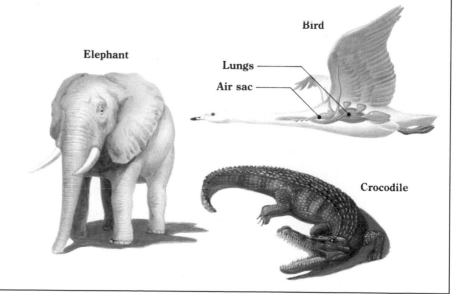

Elephant

Bird

Lungs

Air sac

Crocodile

Were Dinosaurs Social?

Paleontologists are painting a new picture of dinosaur home life. Most modern reptiles mate, lay eggs in solitary nests, and walk away—and scientists always thought dinosaurs did the same. The discovery of two large nesting sites in Montana changed that picture. Adults, young of different ages, eggs, and nests were all found in one small site. At other sites, fossil footprints suggested that some dinosaurs traveled in groups, like herds of bison, while other tracks hinted at a pack of predators all traveling in the same direction. Skeletons at still other sites revealed scenes of pack hunting by small, wolflike flesh-eaters. This evidence leads some scientists to conclude that dinosaurs formed social groups and cared for their young—behaviors never seen in modern reptiles.

A dinosaur "wolf pack" attacks its prey

A pack of *Deinonychus* pulls down a plant-eater. Hunting in packs was thought to be a behavior seen exclusively in mammals until fossilized parts of a 20-foot-long *Tenontosaurus* turned up near the skeletons of three *Deinonychus*. This fearsome, probably warm-blooded predator slashed its prey with a single 5-inch claw on each hind foot. *Deinonychus* stood 5 feet tall and spanned 8 to 11 feet from its snout to the tip of its stiff tail.

A herd of giant plant-eaters

Fossil tracks reveal many things about how dinosaurs lived. One set of tracks shows 23 sauropods—giant, plant-eating dinosaurs—traveling in a herd. Both adults and young traveled in the herd, but adult tracks surround the smaller ones, as if the adults were protecting their young. Because no skeletons turned up nearby, scientists can't be sure which species made the tracks.

A "good-mother" dinosaur feeds her young

Beginning in the summer of 1978, two paleontologists dug up one of the most surprising dinosaur finds of this century. Eventually, more than 300 eggs and 60 skeletons—adults, hatchlings, and juveniles—all came out of a single site. It looked like a dinosaur version of the rookeries formed by penguins and other seabirds. The 3-foot babies were about a month old, but their teeth already showed wear. They had eaten coarse plants, perhaps brought to the nest by the mothers. The scientists named these new hadrosaurs *Maiasaura* (good-mother lizard). Later, another rookery, of a dinosaur named *Orodromeus,* turned up. These dinosaurs had apparently used the same sites year after year.

How Were Dinosaurs Colored?

Models of dinosaurs in museums usually appear in dull, monotone greens, browns, or grays. This is because the fossil record contains very little information about dinosaur colors, leaving scientists almost completely in the dark as to how the creatures looked. However, there are some paleontologists who believe that dinosaurs were vividly colored.

Some evidence for this comes from fossils. For instance, variations in the texture of fossilized dinosaur skin imply distinct color patterns. There are also compelling, if indirect, arguments for color based on what scientists know about modern animals. Factors such as a dinosaur's role in the food chain, its habitat, and its relationship with both other species and the opposite sex of its own species suggest that these reptiles—like contemporary animals—enjoyed wide variations in color.

Colors for different roles

The male *Parasaurolophus,* a type of hadrosaur from the Cretaceous period, had a much longer head crest than the female. Such a physical difference between the sexes might mean that the two sexes had different roles in society. These roles may have been reinforced by color differences.

Colors for warmth

Diplodocus, an 88-foot-long sauropod from the late Jurassic period, probably spent a great deal of time wading in water. As a result, its back may have been darker than the rest of its body in order to better absorb the sun's warming rays as the animal emerged from chilly lakes and rivers.

Colors for protection

Serving as prey for larger and faster dinosaurs, the females and young of the genus *Lambeosaurus* may have benefited from camouflage. The more combative males, with less need for protective coloration, may have sported brighter colors.

What Were Domehead Dinosaurs?

A young male *Pachycephalosaurus* challenges a chief for control of a harem. Only by defeating a chief could a male domehead gain access to females with which he could reproduce.

The largest domehead genus, *Pachycephalosaurus* reached up to 26 feet and roamed the plains of western North America.

Combat consisted of butting heads until either the chief or the challenging male gave up in defeat. The concussion from such impacts would surely have destroyed the creatures' brains and spinal cords were it not for the shock-absorbing design of their skulls, neck ligaments, and vertebrae.

Flourishing in the late Cretaceous period, dome-head dinosaurs had unusually thick skulls. Pale-ontologists believe such hard heads may have enabled the dinosaurs to take part in an elaborate mating ritual, illustrated below.

Male domeheads were territorial creatures that kept harems of females with which they reproduced. When another male challenged the "chief" for control of the harem, the two fought it out by repeatedly butting heads, just as modern-day bighorn sheep do. The dense skulls served to prevent injury as they absorbed the shock of repeated, ferocious impacts.

Domehead skulls and brains

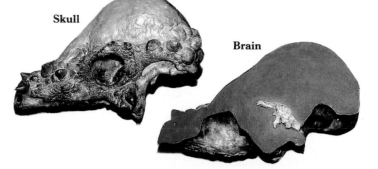

Skull

Brain

Surrounded by bony horns and bumps, the crest of a *Pachycephalosaurus* skull *(top)* was nearly 10 inches thick. Inside the skull, the animal's brain *(bottom, in white)* was only about the size of a sausage.

The victor takes control of the harem while the loser leaves the area. Such battles ensured that only the toughest males reproduced, thereby strengthening the species.

How Did Horned Dinosaurs Evolve?

During the Cretaceous period an order of dinosaurs evolved that was distinguished by unusual heads. The earliest species sported parrotlike beaks, with later arrivals developing large bony frills and long sharp horns. Scientists call such dinosaurs ceratopsians, meaning "horned face."

All ceratopsians were plant-eaters, and their sharp beaks were well suited for breaking off plant leaves and stems. The horns and frills most likely gave protection from predators. When threatened, the creatures could fight back with their horns, which could be more than 3 feet long. The frills, in addition to anchoring strong muscles that made their jaws powerful cutting blades, also protected the creatures' necks, the point at which most predators attack.

A *Triceratops* skeleton fossil shows the massive horns and frills compared with the rest of the skull. *Triceratops* skulls average about 6½ feet from beak to frill.

Leptoceratops had a minimal neck frill and no horns.

Psittacosaurus is the earliest known ceratopsian. Its birdlike beak identifies it as the precursor to horned dinosaurs.

Torosaurus (left), 25 feet long, had the longest neck frill of any ceratopsian.

Pentaceratops had a large frill and three horns. It got its name, which means "five-horned face," because a scientist mistook the reptile's sharp cheekbones for two additional horns.

Styrocosaurus had only one horn. Its frill was short and fringed with sharp spines.

Triceratops, the most famous horned dinosaur, had three horns and a frill.

Protoceratops is the first known ceratopsian with a well-developed neck shield.

How Did Some Reptiles Fly?

The fossil record shows that there were two large groups of pterosaurs, or flying reptiles: rhamphorhynchoids and pterodactyls. Rhamphorhynchoids, characterized by small size and long tails, appeared late in the Triassic period. The late Jurassic period brought the pterodactyls, which were tailless and much larger. The most impressive pterodactyl, *Quetzalcoatlus*, had a wingspan approaching 39 feet and is the largest known flying creature of all time.

For all that is known about them, pterosaurs remain shrouded in mystery. Much remains unknown about how these creatures evolved, flew, and hunted for food.

● *Pteranodon*

The prehistoric equivalent of the albatross, *Pteranodon* was a seafaring pterosaur that fed on fish while flying far offshore.

To take off, *Pteranodon* would sit on a high cliff and launch itself into a current of rising air.

***Pteranodon* flight patterns**

Once airborne, *Pteranodon* would soar as high as it could, then glide down toward the water until the next updraft arrived.

Quetzalcoatlus

Quetzalcoatlus had a long neck, long legs, and a wingspan as wide as a house. Scientists believe that, unlike *Pteranodon,* it may have eaten mollusks and crabs in shallow pools of water.

Pterodactylus

Species from the genus *Pterodactylus* ranged from 10 inches to 8 feet in wingspan. They probably lived mainly off fish.

Pterodaustro

A pterodactyloid with a wingspan of about 52 inches, *Pterodaustro* had teeth that resembled large bristles. It fed by using its teeth to sift small animals from the water.

The puzzle of flight

Fossils of *Quetzalcoatlus* confirm that pterosaurs had evolved specialized bones that were very delicate and virtually hollow. These factors helped keep the creature's weight down to about 160 to 190 pounds, a remarkably low figure for such a large creature.

Even so, an animal this large might not have had muscles strong enough for sustained flight, and scientists were hard-pressed to explain how *Quetzalcoatlus* managed to take off. But in 1985 Dr. Paul MacCready, an American aeronautical engineer, partially solved the problem. Working with members of the Smithsonian Institution's Air and Space Museum, he built a working model of the giant reptile *(right)* that was able to fly by flapping its wings under electrical power.

Which Reptiles Lived in the Sea?

Although no dinosaur species known lived in the sea, there were two groups of Mesozoic reptiles that did—the ichthyosaurs and the plesiosaurs. First appearing during the Triassic period, marine reptiles appear to have evolved from land-bound reptiles whose front and rear legs gradually turned into fins and broad paddles. Some eventually came to resemble fish more than they did reptiles, while others retained a striking resemblance to their terrestrial ancestors.

Stenopterygius was an ichthyosaur that lived during the Jurassic period. It ranged in length from 3 to 7 feet and fed on fish.

Ichthyosaurs and plesiosaurs

Of all marine reptiles, the ichthyosaurs were the best adapted for life in the sea. Built more like fish than reptiles, they had sleek bodies with dorsal (back) and tail fins that made them excellent swimmers. It appears that these creatures lived both close to the shore and far out to sea, just like modern-day porpoises and swordfish.

Plesiosaurs had four paddlelike fins, evolved from legs, that propelled them through the water, much like today's sea lions. Plesiosaurs with long necks, like *Elasmosaurus,* probably lived on the surface of inland seas and dipped their necks underwater to catch fish, while the shorter-necked ones dived to catch their prey.

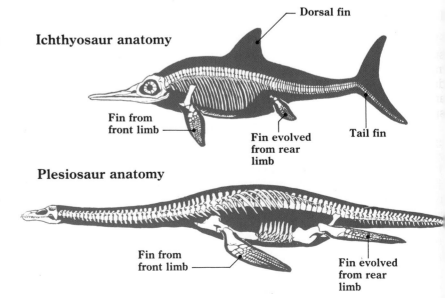

Ichthyosaur anatomy

Dorsal fin

Fin from front limb

Fin evolved from rear limb

Tail fin

Plesiosaur anatomy

Fin from front limb

Fin evolved from rear limb

Elasmosaurus, a plesiosaur of the Cretaceous, lived on fish and squid. Its neck accounted for about half of its 40-foot length.

Ichthyosaur reproduction

How female ichthyosaurs bore young was once the subject of much speculation. Most modern seafaring reptiles, like turtles and alligators, lay eggs on dry land—a method most likely handed down from ancestors on land. When the eggs hatch, the offspring head for the water.

It is unlikely, however, that ichthyosaurs laid eggs on land because their fins would have been virtually useless for crawling even the shortest distance ashore. Rather, scientists have evidence that ichthyosaur eggs developed and hatched within the mother's womb, with the young emerging alive. The discovery of fossils that show tiny ichthyosaur skeletons inside larger ones supports this theory. One rare ichthyosaur specimen is preserved in the process of giving live birth.

What Were Marine Lizards Like?

The latter part of the Cretaceous period marked the appearance of the mosasaurs, a family of sea-faring lizards closely related to the modern-day monitor lizards. Strong swimmers that sometimes grew to over 30 feet, mosasaurs had powerful jaws lined with sharp, fanglike teeth. They used these jaws to feed on both fish and an extinct order of hard-shelled mollusks called ammonites.

Mosasaurs employed their strong jaws to prey on swimming mollusks.

Ammonite shells and mosasaur diet

Mosasaurs fed on ammonites by crushing their shells and eating the soft animal inside. In fact, many fossilized ammonite shells, such as the one at right, bear the distinctive bite marks of mosasaurs.

Mosasaurs fed mainly on fish and had to be fast to catch them. In fact, mosasaurs represent a rapid adaptation from life on land to a life spent entirely in the ocean as a response to the increase in bony fishes. In turn the evolution of ammonites in the late Cretaceous period may have been driven in part by selection in favor of the faster-swimming ones that could escape mosasaurs.

Mosasaur tooth marks

Ammonite shell with bite marks

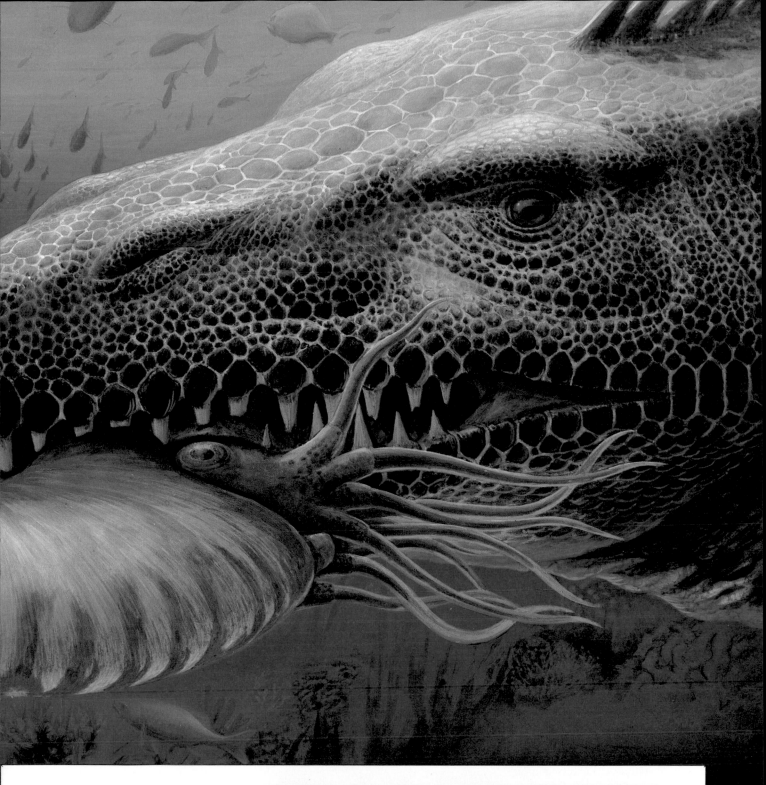

From ammonites to belemnites

Along with ammonites, another group
of now-extinct mollusks flourished
during the Jurassic and Cretaceous
periods. Called belemnites, these
creatures had hard outer shells and
many arms tipped with horny hooks.

Just as ammonites served as prey
for mosasaurs, belemnites were food
for ichthyosaurs *(pages 92-93)*. Scientists have been able to establish this
because many ichthyosaur fossils contain the telltale arm hooks of belemnites. One fossil, discovered in Ger-
many, contained some 478,000
arm hooks—the remains of nearly
1,600 belemnites.

Did Dinosaurs Have Scaly Skin?

Unlike bones, animal skin is soft tissue and virtually never lasts long enough after a creature's death to fossilize. But from the rare fossils that do exist, as well as the less rare fossil imprints of dinosaur skin, scientists have learned something about the look and composition of the skin of dinosaurs and other reptiles.

Most fossils confirm what was believed all along: In the main, prehistoric reptiles had the rough, scaly skin of modern-day alligators and lizards. But some finds were unexpected. Certain specialized reptiles appear to have had equally specialized skin. For example, some marine reptiles had very smooth skin, while flying reptiles may have even had hair on their bodies.

Sordes. Fossils of this pterosaur bear the imprint of hairlike structures, possibly evidence that flying reptiles were warm-blooded.

Ichthyosaurs. While no imprints or skin samples exist, the sleek outlines of ichthyosaur fossils suggest a smooth, slippery skin like that of porpoises.

Tyrannosaurus. The king of flesh-eaters had scaly skin and two rows of bony plates that ran down its back.

Euoplocephalus. Tough plates covered the back of this armored dinosaur. These plates were studded with bony bumps that sharpened into spikes at the shoulders, back of the head, and tail.

The evolution of dinosaur skin

Shown at right is a sample of fossilized dinosaur skin. Dinosaurs arose from the thecodonts, a primitive order of Triassic reptiles. Over time, the scales that covered the thecodonts grew larger and tougher, ultimately becoming the tough, leathery skin found on dinosaurs. In some dinosaurs, like the armored *Euoplocephalus,* the skin became highly specialized, forming bony plates and sharp spines.

What Were Ammonites?

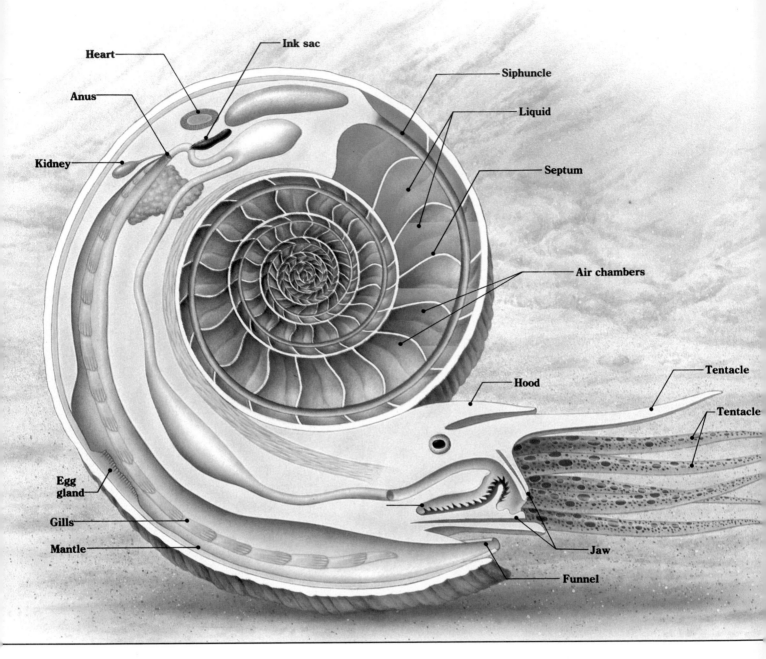

Heart

Ink sac

Siphuncle

Anus

Liquid

Kidney

Septum

Air chambers

Tentacle

Hood

Tentacle

Egg gland

Gills

Mantle

Jaw

Funnel

The shell game

Shown at right are the fossils of two coiled ammonites from the late Cretaceous period. Scientists have long puzzled over the strange shapes of some deepwater ammonite shells. Originally, researchers thought the animals were simply unable to control their shell growth. But recently computer analysis has shown that these bizarre arrangements had a purpose, representing regular—if complex—patterns that may have eased life on the seafloor.

Ammonites were a type of shellfish that appeared in the Paleozoic era and vanished by the end of the Mesozoic era. Their closest modern relatives include the squid, the octopus, and the nautiloids. Fossil shells show that they had features later found in all three living relatives.

Ammonites lived in shells similar to those of the modern chambered nautilus. As an ammonite outgrew its shell, it would seal off the chamber in which it lived and build a bigger one. As chambers built up, the shell grew. The shells of some ammonites grew in a spiral. Others grew in a straight line, and still others took on twisted shapes.

Ammonites, such as the one at left, swam rapidly, moving by shooting water from an organ called a funnel. Fossils of ammonites have been found all over the world.

Spiny, bumpy, or ridged shells probably served to defeat attacks by shell crushers, such as mosasaurs.

Sponging off sponges

Sponge

Fossils indicate that some ammonites may have lived inside sponges. Such an arrangement would protect the ammonites from predators while allowing them to eat food from the water pumped through the sponges' canal systems.

Ammonites and nautiloids

The graceful spiral of this fossil ammonite reveals buoyancy chambers filled with calcite.

Because certain species of ammonites (here, a fossil group from the late Jurassic) appear only in specific geological formations, they enable accurate dating.

The fast-swimming chambered nautilus (here, a specimen from Papua New Guinea) is a modern relative of ammonites.

How Did Prehistoric Birds Live?

Birds represent a remarkable branch in the evolutionary tree of reptiles. Paleontologists believe that these creatures first appeared during the Triassic period, as limbs evolved into wings and reptilian scales gradually turned into feathers. Other ancestral features, such as long, bony tails, remained until the end of the Cretaceous period, when birds began to more closely resemble those that exist today.

Because the bones of primitive birds were hollow and delicate, they are not preserved well in the fossil record. Therefore, scientists know little about the evolutionary history of birds, including how they managed to survive the mass extinctions at the end of the Mesozoic era.

● **An early diving bird**

Hesperornis flourished during the Cretaceous period. A strong swimmer, this bird lived on the water of an inland sea and made its living diving in search of fish. However, its small, hidden wings were not powerful enough for flight.

An early flying bird

Ichthyornis—whose name means "fish bird"—lived onshore but used its strong wings to fly far out to sea in search of fish. Its small, sharp teeth were well suited for grabbing fish from the water in midflight.

What bird skeletons reveal

Working from fossilized skeletons, scientists have divided Cretaceous birds into several categories: Two of them are the hesperorns and the ichthyorns. Hesperorns had well-developed legs and feet but poorly developed wings. They lacked breastbones, necessary for anchoring the muscles required for flight, so were land-bound. Ichthyorns had this skeletal innovation, which allowed them to take to the skies.

The most characteristic feature of all primitive birds was their rows of sharp teeth. A vestige of their reptilian ancestors, the teeth later disappeared as natural selection removed many skeletal features that weighed the birds down.

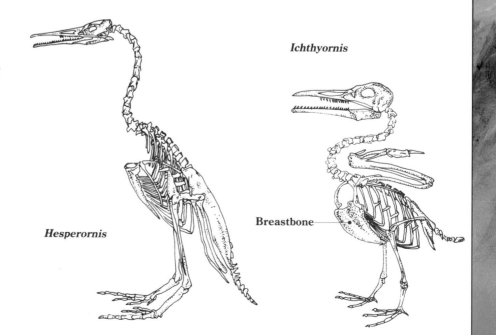

Ichthyornis

Hesperornis

Breastbone

When Did Flowering Plants Appear?

Flowering plants, known scientifically as angiosperms, began to appear during the Cretaceous period. Although their precise phylogeny is unknown, scientists suspect the angiosperms arose from gymnosperms, the most primitive seed-bearing plants.

Angiosperms are one of evolution's most successful experiments. Since their first appearance, over 250,000 species have come into existence, some 200,000 of which are still around. Furthermore, their success has fostered the success of animals, such as insects that feed on plant nectar and herbivores that eat the plants directly.

The Mesozoic bloom

The first seed-bearing plants were gymnosperms, which evolved during the Paleozoic era. These plants had exposed seeds, like those found in the cones of today's pine trees. The illustrations at right show three examples of primitive gymnosperms.

The angiosperm revolution began during the Mesozoic era, as the world exploded with flowers over a very short interval. The fossil record indicates that some of the earliest flowering plants were distant relatives of today's magnolia.

The first ginkgo plants had leaves that fanned out from a single shoot.

Araucaria, a relative of the pines, had large ball-like cones.

Cycadeoidea produced many flowerlike structures on its short and thick stem.

Liriodendron

Evolution of a complex flower

Modern-day angiosperms are probably not much different from some of those of prehistoric times. Today's flowers still produce seeds in structures called pistils, and the seeds are still fertilized by pollen released by organs called stamens. The only major difference is that primitive angiosperms had many pistils per flower (as seen in the modern plant at left), while today's varieties each have many fewer pistils, or only one (as in the modern plant at right).

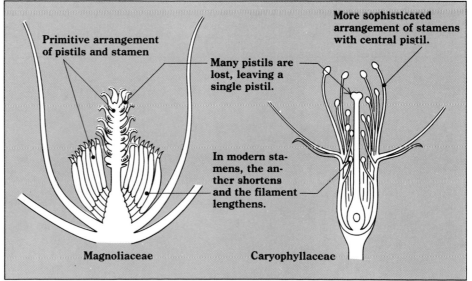

Primitive arrangement of pistils and stamen

Many pistils are lost, leaving a single pistil.

More sophisticated arrangement of stamens with central pistil.

In modern stamens, the anther shortens and the filament lengthens.

Magnoliaceae

Caryophyllaceae

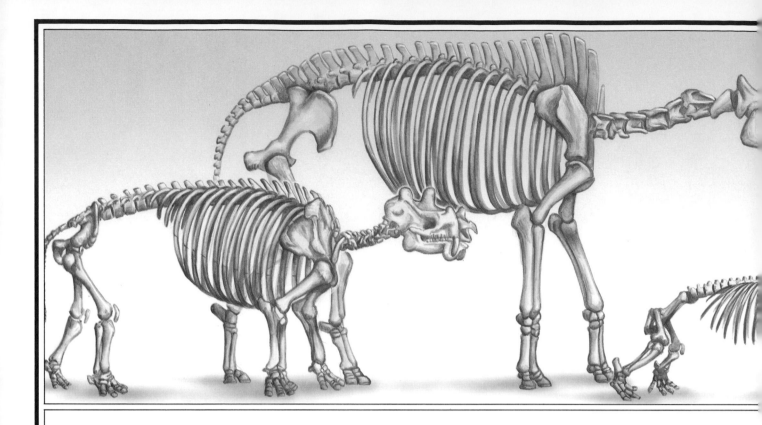

5
The Humans Arrive

The catastrophic events that ended the Mesozoic era 66 million years ago brought the extinction of many plant and animal species but created new opportunities for the survivors. The Cenozoic era could well be called the Age of Birds or Flowering Plants, for they too flourished during the new era. However, human beings understandably prefer to think of the Cenozoic era as the Age of Mammals. Tiny nocturnal mammals had been around since the late Triassic period, but with the disappearance of the dinosaurs, mammals could spread out and take over terri-

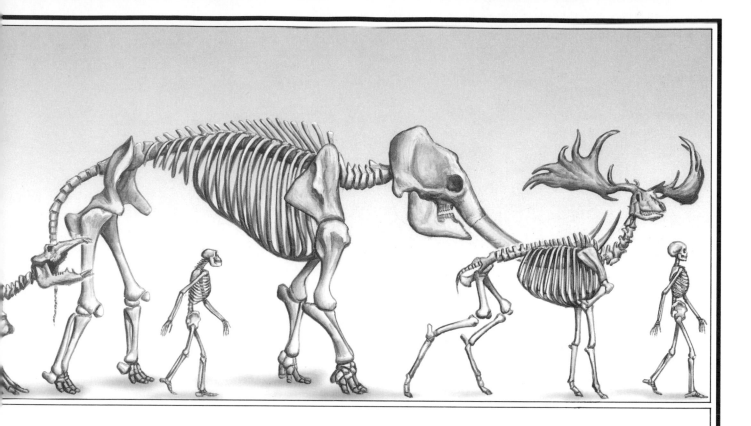

tory that had been vacated by the great reptiles.

In the ocean, advanced bony fishes, or teleosts, became the dominant life form. The great variety of higher teleosts ranges from catfish and sea horses to eels and flying fish. On land, the angiosperms, or flowering plants, flourished. These plants relied on insects to spread their pollen for reproduction, bringing about many new species of both plants and insects. Similarly, new varieties of trees, shrubs, and grasses provided a rich and varied diet for browsing mammals, which in turn spread the seeds of the plants.

In the late Cenozoic era, the Quaternary period has been a time of rapid changes in climate. Ice ages have alternated with warmer intervals, spurring evolutionary adaptations that have led to the plant and animal species that exist today—including human beings.

Skeletons of Cenozoic mammals include *(top, from left)* *Uintatherium, Indricotherium, Desmostylus,* woolly mammoth, *Australopithecus, Megaloceros,* and *Homo sapiens* (modern humans).

What Were the Giant Birds of Prey?

The disappearance of the dinosaurs left a vacancy at the top of the food chain, the spot formerly held by such fearsome predators as *Tyrannosaurus rex*. For a time during the Cenozoic era, giant flightless birds of prey were the dominant flesh-eaters on land. Mammals were still small and provided easy meals for immense predators such as *Diatryma (below)*, which roamed the plains of North America and Europe from the Paleocene through the Eocene epochs.

With their huge beaks, hooked for tearing like a modern eagle's, their powerful legs and deadly clawed toes, *Diatryma* and its relatives had little to fear from other predators of the early Cenozoic era. However, as mammalian evolution proceeded, the earthbound birds of prey became vulnerable to a host of threats. Mammalian predators, with their greater speed and larger brains, competed successfully with the giant birds.

As the climate became drier and cooler, forests gradually gave way to open plains. *Diatryma* was flushed out into the open, and it was in this way that it might have lost out eventually to the shrewd, swift mammals.

● **Diatryma**

Between about 57 million and 40 million years ago, *Diatryma* reigned supreme on the scrubby plains of North America. Standing 7 feet high, with a skull almost as big as that of a modern horse, these birds were flightless but able to run fast. Living singly or in pairs, they preyed on small herbivores such as *Hyracotherium (shown captured below)*, an ancestor of the modern horse. *Diatryma* would outrun its prey, then kill it with one snap of its hooked beak or a kick from its mighty legs.

● *Phororhacos,* South America's big bird of prey

Phororhacos, which appeared about 26 million years ago in South America, resembled *Diatryma* but was not directly related to it. Smaller than *Diatryma,* with a skull 19 inches long, *Phororhacos* may have pecked at its prey in much the same way as a chicken pecks at an insect. Extremely prolific, this large feathered predator flourished in the grasslands of Patagonia until about 7 million years ago.

Sharp-toothed competition

Saber-toothed cats were among the evolving mammalian carnivores that led to the downfall of the giant birds of prey. The size of lions, saber-toothed cats lived in North America until the Pleistocene epoch.

Thylacosmilus of South America resembled a saber-toothed cat, but was actually a marsupial, nurturing its young in a pouch. It stabbed its prey with the long canine teeth growing from its upper jaw.

What Did Early Horses Look Like?

The modern horse is a large plant-eater, standing about 5 feet high at the shoulder. Its earliest ancestor was the much smaller *Hyracotherium,* formerly called *Eohippus,* or "dawn horse." *Hyracotherium* evolved in North American and European forests about 55 million years ago in the Eocene epoch.

As the continents became drier and cooler, jungles gave way to forests, which in turn gave way to grasslands. No longer able to hide among trees, browsing horses were flushed out into open country. Those that could outrun predators lived to reproduce and pass on their helpful features, such as long legs.

The horse's evolution, traced on these pages, is easiest to see in the changes in the structure of its toes *(pink circles).* Over millions of years, the third or middle toe on each foot has gained size and strength, while the other toes diminished. The toenail has evolved into a hoof that envelops the toe and is well suited for supporting the horse as it gallops over grassy plains.

1 *Hyracotherium.* About the size of a modern fox, *Hyracotherium (right)* appeared about 55 million years ago. It had four toes on the front feet and three on the hind, and most of its weight was carried by soft pads similar to a dog's. Its teeth were adapted to eating the soft leaves and fruit of its woodland habitat.

Four toes. The foreleg of *Hyracotherium* ended in four toes. It lacked a big (first) toe, and the third toe was enlarged.

2 *Mesohippus.* Living in North American forests about 35 million years ago, *Mesohippus* stood about 20 inches high and probably ate the young leaves of shrubs and the leaves and pulpy fruits of small trees. Its small teeth and jaw reflected its soft diet. As horses evolved, their teeth and jaws grew larger when their diet changed to include tough grasses.

Three toes. The foreleg of *Mesohippus* ended in three toes that still had pads like a dog's paws have.

3 **Parahippus.** Evolving from *Mesohippus* and the larger *Miohippus* 25 million years ago, *Parahippus* moved from the forests onto North American grasslands. There the longer-legged horses could escape predators, so evolution selected for taller horses.

Big center toe. *Parahippus* had a very large third toe and two small toes that did not touch the ground as it ran.

4 **Pliohippus.** Roaming the North American plains some 12 million years ago, *Pliohippus (right)* had nearly completed the evolution from the four-toed foot of its ancestors to a single-toed hoof.

Single toe. The foreleg of *Pliohippus* resembled that of today's horse, with only a single hoof.

Hoof. The foreleg of *Equus* has a single large toe, reinforced on either side for strength and speed.

5 **Equus, the modern horse.** Evolving about 3.4 million years ago, *Equus* first appeared in North America and then migrated to Asia, South America, Europe, and Africa.

109

How Did Elephants Develop?

Moeritherium *(left)* inhabited North Africa in the late Eocene epoch. The size of a tapir, it fed on grasses at the water's edge.

Gomphotherium *(below)* spread to Europe, Asia, and North America by the late Miocene epoch.

Deinotherium, 10 feet at the shoulder, may have used its tusks to uproot plants, and lived until the early Pleistocene epoch.

Phiomia flourished in North Africa during the Oligocene epoch. Standing 4 feet at the shoulder, it fed on soft plants growing by lakes and rivers.

- **Evolving skulls of elephants**

Moeritherium had a long head, simple molars, and long tusklike incisors.

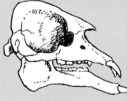

Phiomia had well-developed tusks and a skull similar to a modern elephant's.

Platybelodon—a mastodon found in Asia, Africa, and North America in the mid-Miocene epoch—used its tusks to shovel out vegetation.

Anancus *(below)* lived in the forests of Europe and Asia until the early Pleistocene epoch. Its tusks were up to 10 feet long.

Gomphotherium featured a long skull and tusks extending from both jaws.

The woolly mammoth had big complex molars, used for grazing and grinding.

The African elephant and its slightly smaller cousin, the Indian elephant, are the last survivors of a once-widespread family of herbivores that first appeared on Earth 50 million years ago, in the Eocene epoch.

Early proboscideans (an order that includes both elephants and mastodons) included compact creatures such as *Moeritherium,* which was about 2 feet high at the shoulder. This order evolved into many species of large animals with prominent tusks and a long snout, or trunk. The largest recorded fossil elephant, a species of mammoth, stood 15 feet high at the shoulder and may have weighed 20 tons. The largest modern elephant measures 13 feet and weighs 13 tons. Elephants maintain close-knit family groups with a complex social structure and are highly intelligent. The destruction of habitat and the slaughter by ivory hunters, however, have pushed elephants to the brink of extinction.

Stegodon inhabited East Asia until mid-Pleistocene times. Six to 10 feet high, it had large tusks.

The American mastodon lived in North America from mid-Pleistocene to Holocene times. Males were 10 feet high at the shoulder.

The fur-covered woolly mammoth lived in cool northern climates. Hunted by humans, it died out 12,000 years ago.

The Nauman elephant *(right)* lived in East Asia and Japan until the end of the Pleistocene epoch. This ancient forest dweller stood 8 to 11 feet high.

What Were the Whale's Ancestors?

The blue whale is the largest creature ever to have lived. Yet this 100-foot, 130-ton behemoth, like all whales, evolved from a land omnivore about the size of a fox. These land-mammal ancestors took to the sea by the early Eocene epoch and adapted to aquatic life. Despite evolutionary changes, such as the transformation of forelimbs and tails into flippers, whales retain many traits of their ancestors, such as breathing air and suckling their young.

One cetacean suborder, Archaeoceti, became extinct long ago. Many species of the two surviving suborders, toothed whales and baleen whales, are seriously threatened.

Whales' distant relatives

Although the exact lineage of whales is uncertain, the mammals are thought to be related to Condylarthra, an order of land omnivores. One member, *Andrewsarchus (right),* had a 34-inch skull, and a body perhaps 12 feet long and 6 feet high. The smaller *Mesonyx (far right)* inhabited North America in the Eocene epoch.

Andrewsarchus   *Mesonyx*

Pakicetus, a land-dwelling ancestor

Pakicetus, an ancestor of the whale, probably lived along riverbanks in mid-Eocene times. Fossils show that its inner ear was not fully adapted to withstand the pressure of deep dives, so it probably spent most of its time on the water's surface or on land. As this drawing shows, it may have resembled an otter.

Basilosaurus

Living in the seas of the Eocene epoch, the *Basilosaurus* was a thin, streamlined predator that grew up to 55 feet long. During rapid evolutionary changes, its hind limbs atrophied into vestigial structures.

Whale skull evolution

As the whale's ancestors adapted to the sea, their skulls lengthened, with jaws and teeth extending far forward. Meanwhile, the nostrils moved toward the rear. In modern whales, the nostrils are almost on the top of the head.

Pakicetus had nostrils slightly rearward in the upper jaw. Its teeth included three sets of incisors and three sets of molars.

The jaw of *Basilosaurus* was further elongated, with nostrils farther back toward the eyes. There were now five pairs of molars.

Modern toothed whales have extremely elongated jaws, with nostrils at the top of the head. The teeth are now all conical in shape.

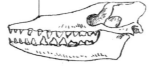

Nostrils

Nostrils

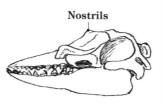

Nostrils

How Did Bats Take Shape?

Of all the many species of mammals, only bats can fly like birds. Bat wings are a modification of both arm and fingers. The bat's patagium, or flying membrane, extends between the shoulder and the hind leg. The bones that support it are the radius, or forearm, and greatly extended bones that correspond to the four fingers of the human hand.

Little is known of the bat's early ancestors. Fossil remains of *Icaronycteris,* an early Eocene bat, are very similar to the bone structure of modern bats. However, the length and width of its wings indicate that this 5-inch-long mammal was a slow flier. The teeth suggest that the ancestral bats were insect-eaters. Most likely, the first bats evolved from small, four-footed land creatures that had gained the ability to glide through the air, the way so-called flying squirrels do.

Because its wings were not fully developed, a transitional bat ancestor would have been an awkward flier and, unlike modern bats, would most likely have hunted ground-dwelling insects.

A gap in the fossil record

No fossil record has been found of the transitional stage when bats began to develop wings. Similarly, little record has been found of the change of whales from land to aquatic creatures. Only a very few creatures die in a manner that results in the preservation of their skeletons, so it is not surprising that there are gaps in the fossil record. According to one theory, evolution may proceed in sudden jumps that punctuate long periods of stability. If this is the case, transition periods may be relatively brief, with few opportunities for intermediate species to be fossilized.

1 **Forebears.** Bats are probably descended from tree-dwelling insect-eaters that flourished after the Cretaceous period.

2 **Gliders.** Early bat ancestors had small patagia and probably glided between trees like modern flying squirrels.

3 **Fliers.** As bats evolved, their patagia enlarged greatly, and bat ancestors probably progressed to true, controlled flight.

4 **Longer "fingers."** As the finger bones in bat ancestors grew longer, their wings grew even larger, allowing them to become more skillful fliers and hunters.

5 **Early true bat.** *Icaronycteris,* a true bat, was found in Lower Eocene strata in Wyoming. The fossil was unusually complete and even included the patagium. The stomach held the remains of insects, probably a typical *Icaronycteris* diet. Except for its primitive teeth, long tail, and lack of breastbone, this animal was very similar to modern bats.

When Did the Biggest Mammals Live?

The first part of the Cenozoic era, called the Tertiary period, began 66 million years ago with the mass extinctions at the end of the Cretaceous period. With the death of the dinosaurs, mammals changed and dispersed as never before, becoming the dominant land animals. While evolution drove some species toward greater speed or intelligence, others, such as those shown here, became huge.

Within 16 million years of the dinosaurs' extinction, mammalian plant-eaters such as *Uintatherium* and *Arsinoitherium* had evolved to take over the land left behind by dinosaurs such as *Triceratops*. After another 20 million years—some 29 million years ago—the largest land mammal ever to have lived, *Indricotherium*, appeared.

● *Uintatherium*

Uintatherium roamed North America during the mid-Eocene epoch. Measuring 11 feet from nose to tail and 5 feet high at the shoulder, it looked like the modern rhinoceros. It had five toes on each foot and three pairs of skin-covered horns. It ate leaves and twigs.

Brontotherium

A large North American mammal of the Oligocene epoch was *Brontotherium*. Although its horns appear to resemble the rhinoceros's horn of modified hair, *Brontotherium*'s horns were formed from bony tissue and probably were covered with skin.

Arsinoitherium

An inhabitant of North Africa during the Oligocene epoch, *Arsinoitherium (below)* was about 10 feet long and had four toes on each foot. It is thought to be related to elephants.

Indricotherium

The largest land mammal ever, *Indricotherium (above)* lived in central Asia from late Eocene to Miocene times. It stood 18 feet high at the shoulder and browsed on treetop leaves other animals could not reach. Although its habits resembled a giraffe's, *Indricotherium* was kin to the rhinoceros.

What Was *Desmostylus*?

At home on land or in the water, *Desmostylus* was a large mammal that resembled a large, four-legged seal and lived from the late Oligocene to the mid-Pliocene epochs. Fossils of the 10-foot-long plant-eaters have been discovered around the Pacific Basin, from California to Japan.

Desmostylus was notable for its unusual molars, which were each formed of a bundle of six smaller cylinders. The animal's name, which means "linked pillars," is based on these distinctive teeth. *Desmostylus* may have used its molars to feed on marine algae. Elephants and manatees are thought to be close modern relatives of *Desmostylus*.

A set of "linked pillars"

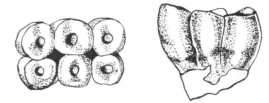

Two views of a *Desmostylus* molar *(above)* show it was a bundle of six smaller, cylindrical columns—looking like pipes welded together.

Family tree of *Desmostylus*

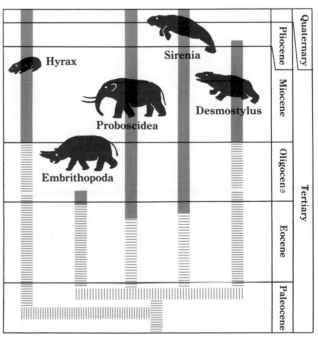

From the shape of its teeth and jaw, scientists believe *Desmostylus* shared a common ancestor with the orders Proboscidea (elephants and mastodons), Sirenia (manatee and dugong), and Hyracoidea (hyrax), as charted above. The survivors of these orders are rare today but were common in the Miocene epoch.

What Mammals Lived in South America?

South American mammals

Pyrotherium, an Oligocene mammal that stood 6 feet high at the shoulder, resembled the elephant but was not related to it.

Glyptodon was encased in body armor from its head to its tail.

Theosodon (below), related to *Macrauchenia*, lived into Pliocene years.

Trigodon was a noto-ungulate—a type of plant-eating mammal—that lived in the Pliocene epoch.

Macrauchenia lived in the Pliocene and Pleistocene epochs. It probably used its long snout for browsing on the plains of Patagonia.

Astrapotherium led an aquatic life during the Oligocene and Miocene epochs.

Didolodus, 5 feet long, was a primitive ungulate of the early Eocene epoch.

Toxodon, about 9 feet long, lived in and out of the water.

Thylacosmilus was a flesh-eating marsupial of the late Miocene to early Pliocene epochs. About 4 feet long, it resembled big cats.

Boryhaena was a flesh-eating marsupial common in the Oligocene and early Miocene epochs. About 3 feet long, it was a successful species.

Many unique mammals evolved in South America during the Tertiary period, when the continent was isolated from the rest of the world (center map). To the left of the maps are mammals that evolved only in South America. Most were placid plant-eaters; certain marsupials were flesh-eaters, taking over the top of the food chain in the absence of other large predators. But in the Quaternary period, a land bridge (bottom map) linked South America to North America. Over this bridge came a host of new mammals, shown to the right of the maps, among them the big cats and other skilled carnivores that hunted many South American mammals to extinction.

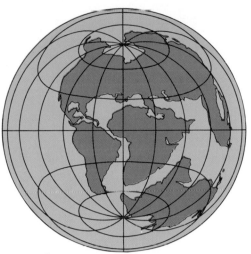

In the mid-Cretaceous period, the southern supercontinent Gondwana split apart, separating South America from Africa.

Thoatherium, which lived until the Miocene epoch, was just 28 inches in length.

In the Paleocene epoch, South America's mammals evolved in isolation from those on other continents.

Invaders from North America

Palaelama, a relative of the camel family, became extinct just 17,000 years ago.

Equus, the modern genus of horse, made its home in South America until 8,000 years ago.

Smilodon, the saber-toothed cat, reached South America in the Pleistocene epoch.

Canis—in this case a bear dog lived in the Americas during the late Miocene and early Pliocene epochs.

In Quaternary times, South America was linked to North America. Animals intermingled.

Cuvieronius was a Pleistocene mastodon, which stood 10 feet at the shoulder.

How Did Primates Evolve?

1 ***Plesiadapis*** was a squirrel-size inhabitant of Paleocene Europe and North America. Because it had claws instead of nails, it could not grasp branches as later primates did.

2 ***Adapis*** inhabited Europe and North America in the Eocene epoch. About 16 inches long, it ate young treetop leaves. The eyes of the *Adapis* were located at the front of its head.

3 **Necrolemur,** found in Europe during the Eocene epoch, had a small body but large eyes and ears. Fleshy mounds on its palms and the bottoms of its feet gave it a good grasp.

4 ***Dolichocebus*** was an ancestor of the New World monkeys. The size of a squirrel, with digits ending in claws instead of nails, it inhabited South America during the Oligocene epoch.

5 ***Mesopithecus*** lived in Greece and Asia Minor during the Miocene epoch. An ancestor of the colobin monkeys, it had a long tail, nimble fingers, and a comparatively large brain.

6 ***Dryopithecus,*** an ancestor of apes, inhabited Asia and Europe during the Miocene epoch. A tailless anthropoid, it lived on the ground and resembled a small chimpanzee.

The primate family, including apes and lemurs, monkeys and humans, evolved from small insectivores similar to today's mole and the shrew some 70 million years ago. *Plesiadapis,* one of the oldest known primates, resembled a rodent. Equally at home in trees or on the ground, it ate fruits and leaves.

As other mammals began to flourish on the ground, the primates took refuge in the trees. Their treetop lifestyle led to a number of impor-tant evolutionary changes. Claws became the flat nails that distinguish all primates. Eyes at the front of the head and improved vision made it easier to judge distance between branches. Color vision developed, aiding the search for ripe fruit. The primates' sense of smell diminished, but their intelligence increased with the development of the cerebral cortex. The primates that finally descended from the trees were bigger, stronger, and smarter than their ancestors.

What Were the Ancestors of Humans?

African ancestor?

Proconsul, a genus of apelike creatures that lived in the Miocene epoch, probably made its home in trees and ate fruit. The different species could be as small as baboons or as bulky as gorillas and walked on all fours *(below). Proconsul* was not exactly like any modern ape, but it had the backbone and brain of a gibbon, shoulders like those of chimpanzees, and wrists like those of monkeys. It may have been an ancestor of all modern apes and of human beings as well.

The first fossil evidence of this animal was found in 1927; the first skull was discovered in East Africa in 1948 by Mary Leakey, wife of noted anthropologist Louis Leakey.

Australopithecus—southern ape

One of the species of *Australopithecus*—scientists aren't sure which one—is believed to be a direct ancestor of humans. The genus appeared some 5 million years ago, stood about 42 inches tall, and had a brain about as big as a chimpanzee's. *Australopithecus* walked upright and may have used tools, but probably could not talk.

Five million years ago, a creature with long arms and a sloping forehead walked upright in the savannas of southern and eastern Africa. This was *Australopithecus.* For 2.5 million years, various species of this early hominid thrived. Some species eventually died out; but one line probably gave rise to *Homo habilis,* whose descendants are reading this book.

But the question of how the ancestors of human beings developed is still open and highly controversial. Many details of human ancestry are missing, and scientists must often revise their theories to fit newly discovered fossil evidence. It does seem clear that a common ancestor, which probably lived in Africa, gave rise to both apes and humans. Unfortunately, no fossils have yet been found that show exactly how these ancient creatures evolved.

Homo habilis—handy human

Evolving about 2 million years ago, *Homo habilis* ("human skilled with tools") made and used tools, beginning perhaps with the simple stone below. With a large brain and dextrous hands, *Homo habilis* lived a wandering life in the savannas of East Africa, eating meat, which it may have trapped, fruits, and vegetables.

How Did Human Beings Evolve?

Homo erectus

Unlike *Homo habilis*, whose fossil remains have been found only in Africa, the fossils of *Homo erectus* have been found from Africa to China and Java, Indonesia. *Homo erectus* stood upright and may have been as tall as modern people. With a brain 50 to 80 cubic inches large, *Homo erectus* was quite intelligent, had mastered the use of fire, and maintained a complex social structure.

The use of fire set *Homo erectus* apart from all the species that had come before. Charred animal bones have been found at *Homo erectus* sites in Africa, China, and elsewhere.

Extinct hominids

Several hominid species evolved in the past few million years, but only one—*Homo sapiens sapiens (far right)*—has survived. As hominids became larger and more erect, their brain size grew dramatically, enabling them to make and use tools, master fire, and form stable and complex social orders.

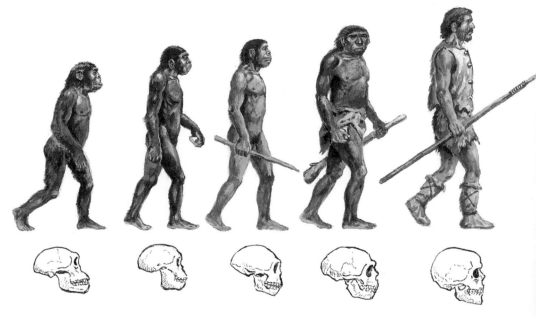

Australopithecus   *Homo habilis*   *Homo erectus*   *Homo sapiens neanderthalensis*   *Homo sapiens sapiens*

The early hominids such as *Australopithecus* and *Homo habilis* appeared in Africa some 2 million to 5 million years ago. By about a million years ago, *Australopithecus* had become extinct; *Homo habilis* was succeeded by the taller, smarter *Homo erectus*.

Homo erectus was a traveler; as its population expanded in Africa, the species gradually ran out of living space. The adaptable hominids then moved beyond the borders of Africa to Asia. *Homo erectus* introduced some dramatic developments in human evolution. One such development was the skilled use of stone tools, articles that had been carefully refined for special uses. The advent of crafted tools also may mean that these hominids were capable of abstract thought. Another milestone was the use of fire, which may have allowed *Homo erectus* to eat formerly inedible food. The third key development was language, giving *Homo erectus* the ability to pass on knowledge to new generations. The stage was set for the appearance of *Homo sapiens*, which included Cro-Magnons, and then for the development of the modern human, *Homo sapiens sapiens*.

The hunt was an important part of the life of *Homo erectus*. Even large animals could be brought down by groups of hunters who worked as a team.

Homo sapiens neanderthalensis

Neanderthals appeared about 150,000 years ago and became extinct just 35,000 years ago. Neanderthals, with brains as large as those of modern humans, performed ritual burials, implying an ability to deal with abstract concepts.

Homo sapiens sapiens

Anatomically modern humans appeared in Africa about 100,000 years ago, migrating to Europe by about 40,000 years ago. The shaped flint tools and rock paintings they left behind indicate that these early humans had a highly developed culture and were skilled hunters.

What Happened during the Ice Ages?

Earth has seen many ice ages—times when huge glaciers accumulate, reaching out from the polar icecaps to cover vast areas of land. During ice ages, warm intervals, or interglacials, occur and the glaciers melt. The latest ice age began some 1.5 million years ago. Four glacial intervals occurred, separated by three interglacials. Earth entered the present warm interglacial interval about 10,000 years ago.

The huge ice sheets that covered much of North America, Asia, and Europe held a lot of Earth's water. Sea levels dropped, exposing a land bridge between Siberia and Alaska, a place where there was no glacier. Many species, including those shown here, migrated over the land bridge between the continents. The migrants included early humans, who reached North America no later than 12,000 years ago.

Early humans in Asia and North America hunted the woolly mammoth. Covered by long hair suitable for cold climates, the woolly mammoth had long, curved tusks with which it may have swept away the snow that covered grasses. By studying the stomach of a virtually intact woolly mammoth frozen in the Siberian permafrost, scientists learned that mammoths lived mainly on grasses and tundra plants. The mammoth was worthy of its name, standing 11½ feet high at the shoulder.

Pleistocene Ice Age

Ice sheets as much as a mile thick covered much of North America, Asia, and Europe *(above)* during the most recent ice age. Around the glaciers' edges, many animals adapted and thrived in a tundra environment like that of present-day Alaska. Trees such as willows and pines grew in sheltered valleys, giving food and cover to many species. Although the latest glacial interval went on for tens of thousands of years, there were probably many warmer spells during which the climate moderated.

The pika is a harelike animal adapted to life in cold, rocky areas. Once widespread, it has survived in Alpine areas since the glaciers retreated.

Megaloceros, an extinct ice-age deer, had antlers measuring 12 feet across. This species lived in Europe, northern Africa, and throughout northern Asia.

The cave lion lived on northern plains. About 6½ feet long, it was larger than today's lion and may have been the same species.

The woolly rhinoceros was a variation on a species that is familiar today. Some 11½ feet long, it fed on grasses and mosses.

The Quaternary ice ages

Modern humans live in the Cenozoic era's Quaternary period, which began about 2 million years ago. In this period, the Earth has had irregular temperature cycles, as shown at right. The valleys on the chart represent major ice ages (shown here with their American names), when large areas of the Northern Hemisphere lay under immense, mile-thick glaciers. In between are warm interglacial intervals *(peaks),* when the ice retreated; modern history has occurred in one such interval.

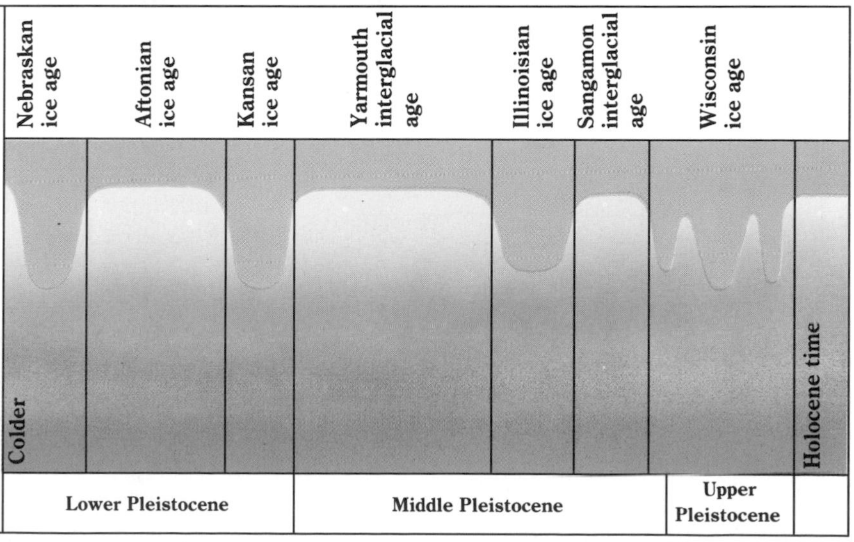

Nebraskan ice age	Aftonian ice age	Kansan ice age	Yarmouth interglacial age	Illinoisian ice age	Sangamon interglacial age	Wisconsin ice age	Holocene time
Colder							
Lower Pleistocene			Middle Pleistocene			Upper Pleistocene	

6
Scientific Proofs of Evolution

Modern evolutionary theory rests not just on the clever speculation of biologists but on a wide base of evidence, collected both before and after Charles Darwin did his important work. Perhaps the strongest evidence of how life evolved comes from fossils. These remains of long-extinct organisms, like windows to the past, help scientists build a rough time line of evolution. The early forms of amphibians, of reptiles, and of mammals can all be traced through fossils and given an approximate date. Groups of fossils, found in layers of sediments accumulated over

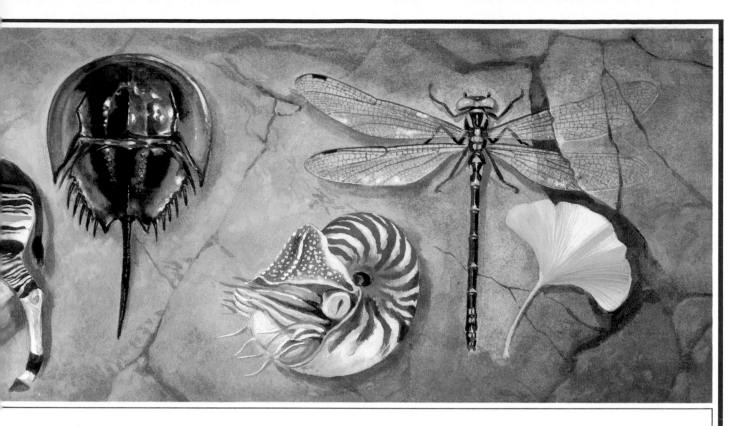

the ages, reveal the details of how organisms gradually changed.

A second line of evidence comes from comparing the anatomies of animals or plants. When different creatures have very similar body structures, they present a powerful argument that the organisms had common ancestors very long ago. For example, the foreleg of a frog, the wing of a bird, and even the flipper of a whale share the same general bone structure as the human arm, though all have been adapted for different uses. Similarities that organisms share during their early development also provide evidence of a common background that only evolution can explain. As embryos, humans and sharks both have gill slits—a reminder of their common heritage. These and other lines of evidence show the great power of modern evolution theory to explain both the links and the dissimilarities among the world's diverse array of creatures.

The modern life forms above still resemble their ancient ancestors. Below, the bat, pteranodon, and pigeon have wing bones similar to those of the human arm.

Why Do Young Organisms Look Alike?

The early stages of an organism's development can give important clues to its evolution and show how closely related it is to other creatures. The shrimp and the barnacle, for example, look very different when fully grown, but the similarity of their immature stages, or larvae, shows that they are related. In the same way, all mammals have common traits early in their development—strong evidence that they evolved from a common ancestor long ago.

Every organism develops in its own way to a mature adult. Animals that are only distantly related begin to look different from one another early on. But the more closely related two animals are, the longer they resemble each other during development.

Shark

Newt

Nereid worm (annelid)

Clam (mollusk)

Crab (arthropod)

Shrimp (arthropod)

Barnacle (arthropod)

■ **Invertebrates**

The barnacle, shrimp, and crab all belong to the arthropod phylum of animals *(blue)*. Their similarities are greatest in their early larval stages; differences in form soon show up as they develop. Clams (in the mollusk phylum) and segmented worms (the annelid phylum) also have similar larvae *(orange)* before their forms diverge.

Turtle

Chicken

Pig

Human

■ **Vertebrates**

Embryos of such diverse animals as the
shark, newt, tortoise, chicken, pig, and human *(above)* are remarkably similar in appearance, attesting to their common heritage.
The evolution of the vertebrates—animals
with backbones—began with fishes and can
be traced through amphibians and reptiles to
modern-day birds and mammals.

M.K

How Are Bat Wings Like Human Arms?

Although outwardly they look very different, the human arm and a bat's wing are remarkably similar in internal structure. The bones of the human arm, hand, and fingers can be matched to comparable structures in the bat's wing. This shows the two species once had a common ancestor.

The two limbs, the bat wing and human arm, are described as homologous. That means they are alike in certain fundamental details, although they may be modified to serve very different functions such as flying or grasping. The wings of modern birds and even of prehistoric flying reptiles are also homologous to the human arm. Identifying and comparing such homologous parts of the body is a key to unraveling the evolutionary history of a species.

The pteranodon wing

The wing in such prehistoric flying reptiles as the pteranodon (below) was a membrane of skin—called the patagium—stretching from the side of the body to the tip of the greatly elongated fourth "finger." Modern-day bats have a similar wing membrane.

The bat wing

In bats, most of the bones corresponding to human fingers have lengthened into a framework for the wing membrane. One finger remains as a claw.

The bird wing

The structure of the bird wing is basically like that of the human arm, but the wrist and finger bones differ considerably. Specialized feathers—not a skin membrane stretched between bones—provide the rigid surface of the wing.

The human arm

The bones and tissues of the human arm are specialized for support rather than for flight. As the fingers and thumb gained greater dexterity, the hand evolved into an efficient tool for holding and handling objects. The shoulder joint gives the arm a wide reach.

Evolution of ear bones

Many homologous organs may appear unrelated at first glance. For example, the bones of the human ear and some bones in a lizard's jaw would not seem to have much in common, yet these bones are, in fact, homologous.

In mammals, the malleus, incus, and stapes carry sound from the middle ear to the inner ear. Fossils of prehistoric reptiles and the earliest mammals *(right)* show how reptilian jawbones evolved into mammals' specialized ear bones.

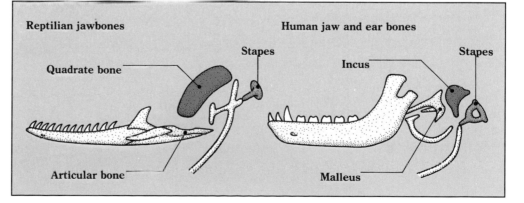

In reptiles, the stapes transmits sound to the ear. The quadrate and articular bones are part of the jaw and do not contribute to hearing.

In mammals, the articular bone has developed into the malleus *(yellow)* and the quadrate into the incus *(red);* the stapes *(blue)* has changed shape.

135

Why Do Unrelated Things Look Alike?

The environment in which a species lives is a powerful influence in helping to shape the outward form of that species. In fact, environment is a key force of evolution. Environmental elements such as the water or food supply, temperature, breeding sites, and other essentials of survival set certain challenges that all species must meet, or migrate or die. It is no surprise, then, that unrelated species in similar habitats often come to resemble one another as they acquire the anatomy best suited to their particular environ-ment. The phenomenon is called convergence.

The three sea creatures below—the dolphin, the swordfish, and the now-extinct ichthyo-saur—belong to three different animal groups. Yet all became fast swimmers by adopting—that is, converging on—a streamlined form that reduced water resistance. In the same way, the desert-dwelling cactus and euphorbia, as well as the insect-catching swallow and swift, have adopted similar forms to meet identical environ-mental challenges.

Streamlined swimmers

The bottle-nosed dolphin is a mam-mal that adapted its front limbs into flippers. Its hind legs have vanished.

The ichthyosaur, a reptile that ap-peared 200 million years ago, had forelimbs modified into flippers and a dorsal fin formed of flesh.

The broadbill swordfish is a true fish, with pectoral, or front, fins that correspond to the front limbs of the dolphin and the ichthyosaur.

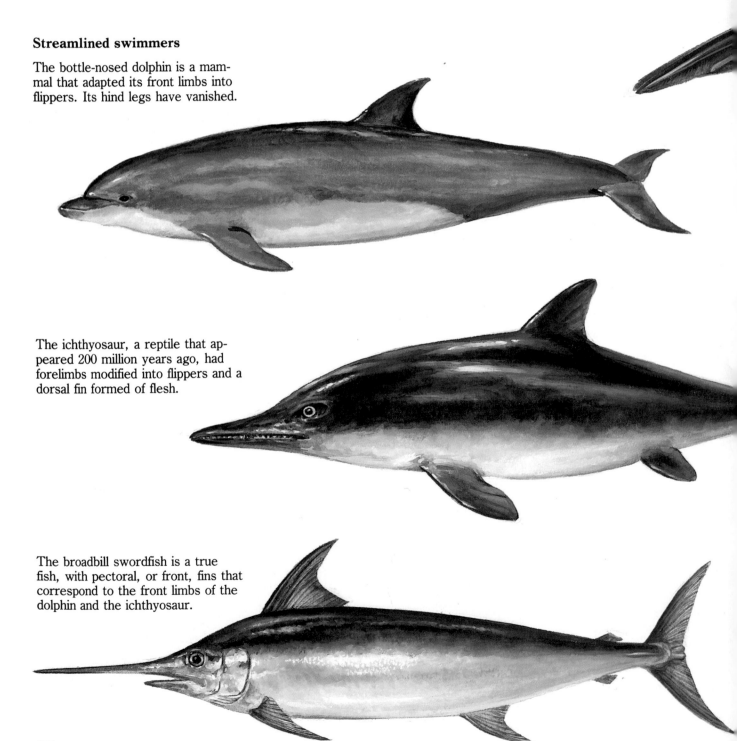

Insect catchers

The swallow has a forked tail and long, slender wings for the speed and maneuverability it needs to catch insects in flight.

The white-rumped swift is only distantly related to the swallow it so closely resembles. Yet it has the same wing structure and its beak, like the swallow's, is wide for catching insects.

Desert dwellers

An American barrel cactus stores water in its thickened stem and has replaced leaves with wilt-proof spines.

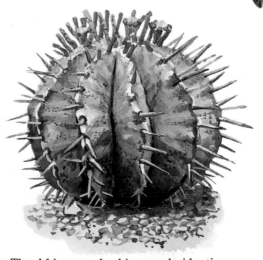

The African euphorbia, nearly identical in form to the cactus, has similar ways of conserving water.

How Did Australian Animals Evolve?

Australia has many marsupials—mammals that nourish their embryonic young in an external pouch, not with an internal placenta like other mammals. More than 100 million years ago, after the earliest marsupials had entered, Australia broke away from other continents. The marsupials spread over Australia, evolving in isolation from other mammals. In a process called adaptive radiation, they evolved many forms and lifestyles to adapt to each new environment they inhabited. Meanwhile placental mammals spread over all the other continents, where most marsupials died out. In a dramatic example of convergence, many members of these two isolated groups came to look and act like each other when they occupied similar, though widely separated, habitats. As this imaginary scene shows, marsupial and placental species (marked with "m" or "pl") can be strikingly similar.

▼ Wolf (pl)

▼ Thylacine (m)

▼ Dasyure (m)

▶ Ocelot (pl)

▼ Marsupial mouse (m)

▲ Shrew (pl)

138

▼ Flying squirrel (pl)

▼ Sugar glider (m)

▼ Wombat (m)

▼ Marmot (pl)

▲ Brush-tailed opossum (m)

▲ Masked palm civet (pl)

▲ Giant anteater (pl)

◄ Numbat (m)

▲ Marsupial mole (m)

▲ Golden mole (pl)

139

What Is a Living Fossil?

Fossils allow scientists to reconstruct the shapes of past organisms and thus trace the tangled paths of evolution. While most species found in fossil form are long extinct, some survive to this day. These are sometimes called living fossils; although they are not literally fossils, they are species that exist seemingly unchanged from their origins millions of years ago. Sixteen such species are shown on these pages.

A living fossil may look like a very early stage in the evolution of other organisms living today. The platypus, for instance, seems to be a very primitive mammal—it still lays eggs, as reptiles do. Some living fossils have remained unchanged by being able to live without competition that forced them to evolve new traits. Others simply still embody the best design for their habitat.

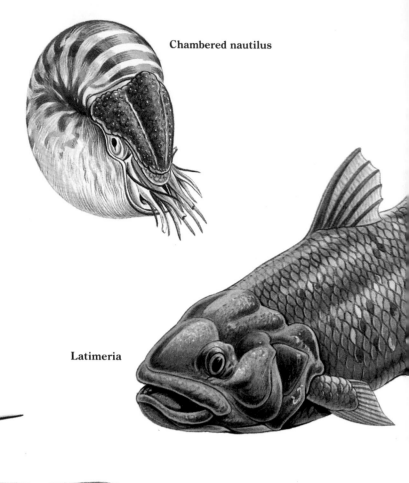

Chambered nautilus

Latimeria

Horseshoe crab

Neoceratodus

Island isolation

Some living fossils owe their longevity to complete isolation from competitors. Islands offer the perfect hideaway for these species. An island's surrounding waters protect such species from others that are evolving in other places and that might cause them to become extinct.

For example, the Ryukyu rabbit *(right)* and the giant tortoise *(far right)* are found only on isolated islands, safe from outside challenge.

The Ryukyu rabbit, whose primitive form resembles the earliest rabbits, inhabits two small islands near Japan.

Giant tortoises survive only in the Aldabra Islands off the coast of Africa and in the Galápagos Islands.

Okapi

Platypus

Onychophoran

Diverse damselfly

Ginkgo

Metasequoia

Ice-age survivors

Many ice ages have punctuated the Earth's long history. During these chilly intervals, numerous species evolved special adaptations to the cold. But a warmer climate put these species at a disadvantage. As the ice retreated, their habitat shrank dramatically. Shown at right are two creatures that survive today by inhabiting only polar and high mountain regions where temperatures are low enough for them.

The pika, which is related to the rabbit, is still a common inhabitant of northern Asia and North America.

The *Parnassius* butterfly requires the colder climes of Alaska, northern Asia, and Europe to survive.

How Do Humans Affect Evolution?

Since life began some 3.5 billion years ago, the great engine of evolution has produced uncounted species, each linked with the past through some of the same DNA, the genetic essence. Today, the familiar factors of competition and natural selection continue to drive evolution, but now a new factor—human activity—has begun to alter the process.

By changing the environment through pollution and overuse, humans have endangered many species—themselves included—making them less fit for survival in today's world. The course of evolution now seems to rely on a different sort of change. Through social evolution, people need to gain the wisdom to live on Earth without destroying it.

The broken chain

As human populations grow and use up natural resources, they may severely damage the delicate workings of evolution within the natural environment.

143

Are Animals Becoming Extinct Now?

As fossils of dinosaurs and other creatures reveal, extinctions have been a natural part of evolution since life began. Now, however, species are being lost more than 100 times faster than if natural causes were the sole reason for their disappearance. Human influences such as overhunting, global pollution, and habitat destruction are the culprits in this deadly trend. Unless people change their destructive habits, many more species will join the extinct animals shown here in the years ahead.

The thylacine, largest of all flesh-eating marsupials, fell victim to a government campaign of destruction by bounty hunters.

The quagga, a zebra species native to South African grasslands, was hunted for both its meat and hide. It disappeared in 1872.

The dodo, a trusting, flightless bird from an Indian Ocean island, was no match for the hungry sailors who relished its tasty meat.

The great auk, native to the islands of the North Atlantic, was slaughtered by the tens of millions for its meat, feathers, and fat.

Steller's sea cow was a docile creature some 30 feet long. Within 27 years of its discovery, people hunted it to extinction.

Glossary

Adaptation: In evolution, an inherited trait that improves an organism's chance of reproduction and survival in its environment.

Adaptive radiation: The process by which many new species arise from a single ancestral group. Each new species is adapted to particular environmental conditions.

Amino acid: One of a group of 20 different types of molecules that are the building blocks of proteins; each is a unique combination of carbon, nitrogen, oxygen, and hydrogen.

Amphibian: A class of cold-blooded vertebrates having moist, smooth skin and four limbs. Amphibians need water for reproduction and use gills for respiration in the early life stages, but use air-breathing lungs as adults.

Ancestor: A plant or an animal from which a species is descended.

Angiosperm: One of two classes of seed plants, angiosperms form flowers and have seeds that develop within a protective structure called a fruit.

Anthropoid: A member of the suborder of primates that includes monkeys, apes, and humans.

Arachnid: A member of a class of arthropods having two body parts, four pairs of legs, and no antennae; includes spiders, ticks, mites, and scorpions.

Arthropod: A member of a phylum of invertebrate animals that have segmented bodies, jointed limbs, and a skeleton on the outside of the body; includes insects, spiders, and crustaceans.

Bacterium: A single-celled, microscopic, prokaryotic organism; the plural is bacteria.

Brachiopod: A phylum of marine invertebrates with a bivalved, or two-part, shell.

Carnivore: A class of flesh-eating mammals including dogs, cats, bears, skunks, otters, and seals.

Cerebral cortex: The outer layer of the brain, where thinking occurs and knowledge accumulates.

Cetacean: An animal belonging to the order of nearly hairless sea-dwelling mammals with paddle-shaped forelimbs; includes whales, dolphins, and porpoises.

Chelicerate: An arthropod with chelicerae, clawlike or fanglike appendages used to manipulate prey; includes spiders, scorpions, and horseshoe crabs.

Chordate: A member of a phylum of animals that at some stage of development have a notochord—a hollow nerve cord located in the back—and paired gill slits. In land-dwelling chordates gill slits are present only in the embryo.

Classification system: An international set of guidelines that allows biologists to name and group organisms by their relationship to other living and fossil things. The broadest category is the kingdom, the narrowest is the species. The categories include kingdom, phylum *(division* is used for plants), class, order, family, genus, and species.

Coelenterate: A phylum of simple aquatic invertebrates that have tentacles and stinging cells; includes jellyfish, hydras, and corals.

Conifer: A cone-bearing seed plant with mostly evergreen needles or scalelike leaves; includes pine trees.

Convergence: Evolution that results in similarities in the physical form of unrelated species sharing the same habitat.

Crinoid: One of a class of animals in the echinoderm phylum having conical, globular, or bowl-shaped bodies with five or more erect branching arms; includes sea lilies and feather stars.

Diapsid: A reptile having a pair of openings in the skull behind each eye socket. The group includes dinosaurs, crocodiles, and snakes.

Differentiation: The process by which isolated members of a species undergo genetic changes and evolve into a separate species.

Dinosaur: A member of a group of extinct, land-dwelling reptiles that flourished between 215 million and 65 million years ago.

Echinoderm: A phylum of marine invertebrate animals having five-sided symmetry, an internal skeleton, a spiny surface, and small suction cups for feeding or locomotion; includes starfish and sea urchins.

Environment: The climate, soil, and living things with which an organism interacts and which determine its form and survival.

Eukaryote: An organism with complex cells containing a membrane-bound nucleus, mitochondria, many chromosomes, and other complex internal structures; one of the two principal types of cells, the other being prokaryotes.

Evolution: Change through time in the diversity and adaptation of populations of organisms.

Extinction: The death of a species that occurs when the last individual of the species dies.

Fossil: Any evidence of life from the geologic past; includes bones, footprints, or entire animals or plants.

Gene: A distinct chemical unit of hereditary material, usually made of DNA, that determines an inherited characteristic and is passed from parent to offspring.

Genetics: The science that studies the ways hereditary information is passed from parent to offspring.

Genus: A group of closely related species.

Gymnosperm: One of a class of seed plants that reproduce without flowers or fruit.

Herbivore: An animal that eats plants or plantlike organisms.

Homologous: A term describing the presence, in two or more different plant or animal groups, of structures that have the same ancestry but serve different functions.

Hybrid: An offspring of two different but closely related varieties or species.

Invertebrate: An animal without a backbone.

Kingdom: The largest category in the classification system; all living and fossil organisms are currently divided into five kingdoms: Monera (bacteria), Protista (one-celled eukaryotes), Fungi, Plantae, and Animalia.

Mammal: A member of a class of warm-blooded vertebrates that are covered with hair or fur and nourish their young with milk from their mammary glands.

Marsupial: One of an order of mammals, including kangaroos and opossums, whose young are born at an immature stage and complete their development in the mother's abdominal pouch.

Mitochondrion: A structure in a eukaryotic cell that releases the energy in food molecules for use by the cell; the plural is mitochondria.

Mollusk: A member of a phylum of invertebrates having soft unsegmented bodies that are often enclosed in a shell; includes clams, snails, and octopuses.

Mutation: A stable and inheritable change in an organism's genes.

Natural selection: The process by which organisms with certain traits survive in a given environment and produce more offspring than organisms with less favorable traits.

Niche: The role played by a species in its ecosystem, including its habitat, feeding activity, interactions with other species, and effects on its surroundings.

Notochord: A flexible, supportive rod of cartilage in lower chordates and in the embryo of higher chordates that runs the length of the body; in higher chordates the vertebral column forms around the notochord.

Nucleic acid: Any of a group of organic acids, consisting of long chains of nucleotides, found in the nucleus of cells. Nucleic acids store genetic information and make possible the manufacture of proteins from amino acids. There are two main types of nucleic acids—DNA, or deoxyribonucleic acid, and RNA, or ribonucleic acid.

Nucleotide: The basic molecular unit of a nucleic acid, consisting of a sugar, a phosphate group, and a nitrogen-containing base.

Omnivore: An animal that eats both plants and animals.

Paleontology: The science that deals with the life of past geologic ages as revealed in fossil remains.

Pangaea: A supercontinent, believed to have existed 300 million to 200 million years ago, that included all present-day major landmasses. Modern continents are thought to have formed when Pangaea broke up.

Population: A group of organisms of the same species that live together in the same region.

Predator: An animal that hunts and eats other animals.

Primate: One of an order of mammals having binocular vision, grasping hands, and flexible feet, each with five digits; includes humans, apes, and monkeys.

Prokaryote: A single-celled organism that contains no nucleus, no mitochondria, and a single circular strand of DNA. It is one of the two principal types of cells, the other being the eukaryote.

Protein: A compound, made of long linked chains of amino acids, found in all living matter.

Reptile: A member of a class of cold-blooded vertebrates having dry scaly skin and internal fertilization of shelled eggs laid on land.

Species: A group of organisms in a population that are structurally similar and that can pass these similarities on to their offspring through reproduction.

Spiracle: A breathing hole or slit in arachnids, insects, sharks, and bony fishes.

Stratum: A single distinct layer of sedimentary rock; the plural is strata.

Therapsid: A member of an order of extinct reptiles that walked upright and are thought to be the ancestors of mammals.

Thorax: In insects and crustaceans, the body region between the head and the abdomen bearing the walking legs and wings.

Trait: In genetics, an inherited characteristic.

Ungulate: A four-legged mammal that walks on hoofs and eats plants; includes horses, rhinoceroses, and giraffes.

Vertebrate: An animal with a backbone.

Vestigial structure: In an organism, a structure that is no longer functional.

Geologic time

Scientists have divided time into different intervals, beginning with Precambrian time, which includes all time from the formation of the Earth until the Paleozoic era. The chart below shows the main time divisions from the Paleozoic on, with eras covering the longest spans of time and epochs the shortest.

Era	Period	Epoch	Years Ago
Cenozoic	Quaternary	Holocene	0 to 10,000
		Pleistocene	10,000 to 2 million
	Tertiary	Pliocene	2-5 million
		Miocene	5-24 million
		Oligocene	24-37 million
		Eocene	37-58 million
		Paleocene	58-66 million
Mesozoic	Cretaceous		66-144 million
	Jurassic		144-208 million
	Triassic		208-245 million
Paleozoic	Permian		245-286 million
	Carboniferous		
	Pennsylvanian		286-315 million
	Mississippian		315-360 million
	Devonian		360-408 million
	Silurian		408-438 million
	Ordovician		438-505 million
	Cambrian		505-570 million

Index

149

Staff for
UNDERSTANDING SCIENCE & NATURE

Assistant Managing Editor: Patricia Daniels
Editorial Directors: Allan Fallow, Karin Kinney
Writer: Mark Galan
Assistant Editor/Research: Elizabeth Thompson
Editorial Assistant: Louisa Potter
Production Manager: Prudence G. Harris
Senior Copy Coordinator: Jill Lai Miller
Copy Coordinator: Juli Duncan
Production: Celia Beattie
Library: Louise D. Forstall
Computer Composition: Deborah G. Tait (Manager),
    Monika D. Thayer, Janet Barnes Syring, Lillian Daniels

Special Contributors, Text: Joseph Alper, Stephen Hart,
    Barbara Mallen, Greg Mock, Mark Washburn
Design/Illustration: Antonio Alcalá, Caroline Brock, Nicholas
    Fasciano, Catherine D. Mason, David Neal Wiseman
Photography: Cover: Tui De Roy Moore/Bruce Coleman. Title
    page: Smithsonian Institution. 50: David R. Schwimmer/Bruce
    Coleman. 51: Breck P. Kent/Earth Scenes. 52: Field Museum
    of Natural History (2). 73: Natural History Museum/
    Smithsonian Institution. 98: Bruce Coleman, photo by Jane
    Burton (top); Sinclair Stammers/Science Photo Library/
    Photo Researchers (middle); Bruce Coleman, photo by Jon
    and Valerie Taylor (bottom).
Research: Jocelyn Lindsay
Index: Barbara L. Klein

Consultant:
Raymond Rye is a museum specialist in the Department of Paleo-
    biology, National Museum of Natural History, Smithsonian
    Institution.

Library of Congress Cataloging-in-Publication Data
Evolution of life / editors of Time-Life Books.
    p.   cm. — (Understanding science & nature)
    Includes index.
    Summary: Questions and answers present information about
the theory and process of evolution.
    ISBN 0-8094-9695-X (trade) — ISBN 0-8094-9696-8 (lib.)
    1. Evolution (Biology)—Miscellanea—Juvenile literature.
[1. Evolution—Miscellanea.   2. Questions and answers.]
I. Time-Life Books.   II. Series.
QH367.1.E96   1992
575—dc20   92-8227
                                             CIP
                                           AC r92

TIME-LIFE for CHILDREN ®

Publisher: Robert H. Smith
Associate Publisher and Managing Editor: Neil Kagan
Assistant Managing Editor: Patricia Daniels
Editorial Directors: Jean Burke Crawford, Allan Fallow,
    Karin Kinney, Sara Mark, Elizabeth Ward
Director of Marketing: Margaret Mooney
Product Managers: Cassandra Ford, Shelley L. Schimkus
Director of Finance: Lisa Peterson
Financial Analyst: Patricia Vanderslice
Administrative Assistant: Barbara A. Jones
Special Contributor: Jacqueline A. Ball

Original English translation by International Editorial Services Inc./
C. E. Berry

First Printing. Printed in Malaysia.
Published simultaneously in Canada.
Time Life Inc. is a wholly owned subsidiary of
THE TIME INC. BOOK COMPANY.
TIME LIFE is a trademark of Time Warner Inc. U.S.A.
For subscription information, call 1-800-621-7026.